# THE MIRROR OF GESTURE

# THE MIRROR OF GESTURE
## BEING THE ABHINAYA DARPANA OF NANDIKESVARA

TRANSLATED INTO ENGLISH

ANANDA COOMARASWAMY
AND
GOPALA KRISTNAYYA DUGGIRALA

GYAN

*Published by*

Gyan Publishing House
5, Ansari Road
Daryaganj, New Delhi-110002
Phone: 011-47034999, 9811692060
E-mail: books@gyanbooks.com

*Distribution Network*
gyanbooks.com
India, USA, Canada, UK, Australia, France



ISBN : 978-81-212-9140-8 (PB)
First Published, 1917

2nd Impression 2023

*Printed at:* Gyan Press, Delhi.



**THE MIRROR OF GESTURE**

TRANSLATORS: ANANDA COOMARASWAMY, GOPALA KRISTNAYYA DUGGIRALA

# THE MIRROR OF GESTURE

## BEING THE ABHINAYA DARPAṆA OF NANDIKEŚVARA

TRANSLATED INTO ENGLISH

BY

ANANDA COOMARASWAMY

AND

GOPALA KRISTNAYYA DUGGIRALA

WITH INTRODUCTION AND ILLUSTRATIONS

CAMBRIDGE
HARVARD UNIVERSITY PRESS
LONDON: HUMPHREY MILFORD
OXFORD UNIVERSITY PRESS
1917

INSCRIBED BY THE TRANSLATORS
WITH AFFECTIONATE GREETING
TO ALL ACTORS AND ACTRESSES

# CONTENTS

## LIST OF PLATES

# THE MIRROR OF GESTURE

## INTRODUCTION

Mr. Gordon Craig, who understands so well the noble artificiality of Indian dramatic technique, has frequently asked me for more detailed information than is yet available in this too long neglected field.

"If there are books of technical instruction," writes Mr. Gordon Craig, "tell them to me I pray you. The day may come when I could afford to have one or two translated for my own private study and assistance. I dread (seeing what it has already done in other arts here) the influence of the finished article of the East; but I crave the instruction of the instructors of the East. The disastrous effect the Chinese porcelain and the Japanese print has had on us in painting we must try to avoid in this theatre art. . . . You know how I reverence and love with all my best the miracles of your land, but I dread for *my* men lest they go blind suddenly attempting to see God's face. You know well what I mean, I think. So I want to cautiously open this precious and dangerous (only to us queer folk) book of technical instruction before the men go crazy over the lovely dancers of the King of Cambodia, before the 'quaintness' tickles them, before they see a short cut to a sensation. If only you knew how unwilling these men of the theatre (most of all those dissatisfied with the old sloppy order) were to face the odds, and how they long to escape obligations (your phrase in 'Sati') you would almost make a yearly tour of England crying 'Shun the East and the mysteries of the East'."[1]

While we still lack a complete and adequate translation, and even a satisfactory edition, of the "Dramatic Science" (*Nāṭya Śāstra*) of Bharata, the present version of a shorter compendium known as the "Mirror of Gesture" (*Abhinaya Darpaṇa*) of Nandikeśvara may be of use as an introduction to Indian method.

The dramatic scriptures of India were framed by Brahmā at the request of the lesser gods, at the very beginning of the Treta Yuga, the last aeon before the present. This event is described as follows in the first chapter of the "Nāṭya Śāstra" of Bharata:

[1] Extract from a letter written in 1915.

When Brahmā was a Sage in the Kṛta Age, and when Vaiśvata Manu was preparing for the Treta Age, when popular morality is in the grasp of greed and of desire, and the world is deluded by envy, by resentment, and by weal and woe, when the Devas, Dānavas, Gandharvas, Yakṣas, Rākṣasas, Mahoragas, and the Lokapālas entered upon Jambu-dvīpa, then Indra and the other Devas said to Brahmā: " We desire a pastime to be seen and heard. This matter of the Four Vedas should not be heard by Śūdras, pray therefore shape another and a fifth Veda for all the castes."

Saying to them, " So let it be," and turning away from Indra, he who knows the essence of every matter, seated in Yoga posture, called to his mind the Four Vedas, thinking, " Let me make a Fifth Veda, to be called Nāṭya (Drama), combined with epic story, tending to virtue, wealth, (pleasure and spiritual freedom), yielding fame—a concise instruction setting forth all the events of the world about to be, containing the significance of every Scripture, and forwarding every art." Thus, recalling all the Vedas, the Blessed Brahmā framed the Nāṭya Veda from the several parts of the Four Vedas, as desired. From the Ṛg Veda he drew forth the words, from the Sāma Veda the singing, from the Yajur Veda gesture, and from the Atharva Veda the flavour.

This science was communicated by Brahmā to Bharata and to his hundred sons, and it was first used at the Flag Festival of Indra, to celebrate the victory of the Devas in battle against the Dānavas. When, however, the Dānavas found that the drama depicted their own defeat, they remonstrated with Brahmā, and this afforded occasion for an explanation of the true character and significance of dramatic art—not to flatter any party, but to represent the true and essential nature of the world. Brahmā explains to the Dānavas:

" This play is not merely for your pleasure or the pleasure of the Devas, but exhibits mood (*bhāva*) for all the Three Worlds. I made this play as following the movement of the world (*loka-ṛt'-anukaraṇam*), whether in work or play, profit, peace, laughter, battle, lust, or slaughter; yielding the fruit of righteousness to those who follow the moral law, pleasure to those who follow lust, a restraint for the unruly, a discipline for the followers of a rule, creating vigour in the impotent, zeal in warriors, wisdom in the ignorant, learning in scholars, affording sport to kings, endurance to the sorrow-smitten, profit to those who seek advantage, courage to the broken-willed; replete with the divers moods (*bhāvas*), informed with the varying passions of the soul, linked to the deeds of all mankind, the best, the middling, and the low, affording excellent counsel, pastime, weal and all else.

This drama shall be the source of all counsel in matters of flavour (*rasa*), mood (*bhāva*), and every rite; it shall serve as a timely resting-place for those who are grieved, weary, unhappy, or engaged in an arduous discipline;

bestowing righteousness, renown, long life, fortune, increase of reason; affording counsel to the world. That which is not to be found herein is not knowledge, nor craft, nor wisdom, nor any art, nor deeds, nor Union (*yoga*).

I made this drama according to the Seven Lands, and so you should not feel resentment towards the Immortals. The drama is to be understood as witnessing the deeds of Gods and Titans, kings of the spheres, and Brahmā-sages. Drama is that which accords with the order (*sva-bhāva*) of the world, with its weal and woe, and it consists in movements of the body and other arts of expression (*abhinaya*). The theatre is such as to afford a means of entertainment in the world, and a place of audience for the Vedas, for philosophy, for history, and other matters."

He adds that no performance should be begun without fulfilling the Office of the Stage (*ranga-pūjaḥ*), and that those who neglect this ritual will be ruined.

In a following chapter Bharata explains, in connection with the building of the theatre, how it is that the behaviour of the artist must of necessity be studied, and not impulsive; for the human actor, who seeks to depict the drama of heaven, is not himself a god, and only attains to perfect art through conscious discipline: "All the activities of the gods, whether in house or garden, spring from a natural disposition of the mind, but all the activities of men result from the conscious working of the will; therefore it is that the details of the actions to be done by men must be carefully prescribed."

Indian acting or dancing — the same word, Nāṭya, covers both ideas — is thus a deliberate art. Nothing is left to chance; the actor no more yields to the impulse of the moment in gesture than in the spoken word. When the curtain rises, indeed, it is too late to begin the making of a new work of art.[1] Precisely as the text of the play remains the same whoever the actor may be, precisely as the score of a musical composition is not varied by whomsoever it may be performed, so there is no reason why an accepted gesture-language (*angikābhinaya*) should be varied with a view to set off advantageously the actor's personality. It is the action, not the actor, which is essential to dramatic art. Under these conditions, of course, there is no room for any amateur upon the stage; in fact, the amateur does not exist in Oriental art.

[1] This general principle holds good even where an author acts his own play.

Granting, of course, a variety of natural capacity, there naturally appears to be less difference between the good and bad actor than we are accustomed to observe in modern Europe, because the actor who merely exhibits *himself* is eliminated altogether. The difference, however, exists, and the Indian connoisseur is as sensitive to every shade of it as the western critic to the wider range of variation on the European stage. The perfect actor has the same complete and calm command of gesture that the puppet showman has over the movements of his puppets; the exhibition of his art is altogether independent of his own emotional condition, and if he is moved by what he represents, he is moved as a spectator, and not as an actor.[1] Excellent acting wears the air of perfect spontaneity, but that is the art which conceals art. It is exactly the same with painting. The Ajaṇṭā frescoes seem to show unstudied gesture and spontaneous pose, but actually there is hardly a position of the hands or of the body which has not a recognized name and a precise significance. The more deeply we penetrate the technique of any typical Oriental art, the more we find that what appears to be individual, impulsive, and 'natural', is actually long-inherited, well-considered, and well-bred. Under these conditions life itself becomes a ritual. The Indian actor relies only to a very small extent on properties, and still less on scenery. Referring to this, Bābu Dinesh Chandra Sen remarks with justice of the Bengālī Yātrās, that these folk-plays "without scenery, without the artistic display of costumes, could rouse emotions which nowadays we scarcely experience while witnessing semi-European performances given on the stages of the Calcutta theatres."[2]

But it is not merely in connection with folk-plays that accessories are needless. Let us take a few episodes from the "Śakuntalā" of Kālidāsa and see how they are presented. The "Watering of a Tree" is to be acted according to the following direction: "First show *Nalina-padmakośa* hands palms downwards, then raise them to the shoulder, incline the head,

[1] "Sāhitya Darpaṇa", 50.

[2] "History of Bengali Language and Literature", 1911, p. 733.

somewhat bending the slender body, and pour out. *Nalina-padmakośa* hands are as follows: *Śukatuṇḍa* hands are crossed palms down, but not touching, turned a little backward, and made *Padmakośa*. To move the *Nalina-padmakośa* hands downwards is said to be 'pouring out'." The action indicated is practically that of the extreme left-hand figure in Plate XII of the India Society's "Ajanta Frescoes" (Oxford, 1915), but the actress, of course, only makes believe to lift and pour, she does not make use of an actual vessel. "Showing Fear of a Bee" is to be acted as follows: "Move the head quickly to and fro (*Vidhutam*), the lips quivering, while *Patāka* hands are held unsteadily against the face, palms inward." "Gathering Flowers" is to be acted as follows: "Hold the left hand horizontally in *Arāla*, the right hand in *Haṃsāsya*, extended forward at the side." The left hand here represents a basket, and imaginary flowers are picked with the right hand and transferred to the left. "Mounting a Car" is to be shown as follows: "The knees are to be raised, the leg being bent and lifted, so that the knee is level with the chest, and there held; and then the same is done with the other foot." [1]

It should be noted throughout that the words *Nāṭya*, etc., imply both acting and dancing; we have used the word 'dance' in our translation only for want of any English word combining the ideas of dancing and acting. The reader will go far astray if he understands by dancing anything but rhythmic shewing. Indian acting is a poetic art, an interpretation of life, while modern European acting, apart from any question of the words, is prose, or imitation.

It is needless to say that the appeal of the Indian actor's art can only be felt by a cultivated audience; it is for this reason that it possesses so little interest for the ordinary European

[1] Śukatuṇḍa, Padmakośa, Arāla and Haṃsāsya hands, and the Vidhuta head are explained in the text of the "Mirror of Gesture" translated below. The above stage directions are from Rāghavabhatta's "Arthadyotanikā", a commentary on Śakuntala, printed in the "Abhijñāna Śakuntalā" edited by Godabole and Paraba, Bombay, 1886. The immediate source is Sylvain Levi's well known and valuable work, "Le Théâtre Indien", which is, however, mainly concerned with the literature, rather than the technique of the Indian drama.

spectator, who remains from beginning to end of the performance — if he remains so long — an outsider. The Indian artist is a professional, and he works for an audience of unsparing critics. The fact that dancing or pantomime is a learned art appears in all the literature, and the accomplished actor must be accomplished in many things. In the "Mirror of Gesture", for example, the various definitions are constantly supported by the remark, "This is the view of those who are learned in the Bharatāgama."[1] It must not be imagined on this account that Indian Nāṭya served or serves only for the entertainment of an academic clique. This may have been the case with the old court dramas, but it was not so with Nāṭya in general, which corresponded to the common and collective need of the folk. Where such a need is felt, there arises a common and collective art, that is to say, an art which is not, indeed, practised by everyone, but is understood by everyone. The Indian actor, despite the apparent complexity of the gesture-language, makes no movement of which the meaning is incomprehensible to an Indian audience, while the subject-matter — religious, epic, or erotic — is common ground for all. But the knowledge of technique and theme is not alone sufficient, without imagination; and according to the Indian view, the power to experience aesthetic emotion is inborn, it cannot be acquired by mere study, being the reward of merit gained in a former life.[2] Whether or not this be true of the individual, it is certainly true of human communities, where no great art ever yet sprang into being out of nothing in a single generation. Art, and the general understanding of art, are always the result of a long, united, and consistently directed effort, and nothing can be done unless the artist and the spectator share a common inspiration. How far this is assumed to be the case in India may be gathered from the remarks of the dramatic critics such as Dhanaṃjaya, who pours scorn upon the spectator who seeks in drama the statement of fact rather than the experience

[1] Phrases of this nature, which are constantly repeated, are generally omitted in our translation.

[2] "Knowledge of Ideal Beauty," says Blake, "is not to be acquired. It is born with us."

of joy,[1] and says that this experience depends upon the spectator's own capacities, and does not arise from the perfections of the hero, or because the work was deliberately designed to create a beautiful effect; it is their own effort by which the audience is delighted, just as in the case of children playing with clay elephants, whose imagination bestows upon their toys a varied and abundant life.[2] Those who lack imagination are said to be no better than furniture, walls, or stones.[3]

The old Indian dramatic art is no longer to be seen in India in a complete state.[4] The art of the modern Parsee theatres, chiefly exhibited in large towns such as Bombay and Calcutta, is only nominally Indian. The scenery and costume are elaborate, incongruous, and tawdry; the music and the ballet hybrid; and the acting, though generally clever, is ill-informed and unsensitive.[5] Authentic Indian acting, however, survives in the 'Nautch', a form of dance which sets forth a given theme by means of song and gesture combined. Performances of this kind do not correspond very closely to modern European conceptions of the dance, which belong rather to what is called in India mere *Nṛtta*, rhythmic movement without a theme and therefore without "flavour." The Indian Nācnī (Nautch-girl, *bayadère*) generally exhibits an alternation of Nṛtta and Nṛtya. The latter, together with the sister art of music, must be regarded as representing the most perfect form of old Indian practical aesthetic culture now surviving, and one of the most beautiful and moving arts that maintain a precarious existence in a world that is

[1] The essential characteristic of aesthetic emotion (*rasāsvādana*) is a timeless delight (*ānanda*) akin to that of the experience of union with the Brahman (*Brahmāsvādana*). — "Sāhitya Darpaṇa", 33, 54.

[2] "Daśarūpa", i, 6, and iv, 47–50 and 90. For the general question of aesthetic emotion, see also the "Sāhitya Darpaṇa" of Viśvanātha Kavirāja, (Calcutta, 1875); Regnaud, "La Rhétorique Sanskrite", Paris, 1884; and my "Hindu View of Art", in "The Quest", 1915, and "That Beauty is a State", Burlington Magazine, 1915.

[3] Dharmadatta, quoted "Sāhitya Darpaṇa", 39.

[4] It survives, perhaps, in Cambodia. Cf. A. Leclère, "Le Théâtre Cambodgien", Revue d'Ethnographie et de Sociologie, 1910, Nos. 11–12, pp. 257–282 — a valuable paper, and well illustrated.

[5] It may be remarked that the few attempts that have so far been made to exhibit Indian drama on the English stage have merited similar criticism.

"thinking of something else." There are still innumerable Indian temples where the ritual dancing of Devadāsīs before the image is a part of the regular daily office; while in orthodox circles the Nautch is still an indispensable element in all festivities such as weddings and coronations. The Nautch is a direct survival of the old Indian Nāṭya. But the material of the classic drama is rarely if ever presented at the present day, the theme of the modern Nautch being most often Vaiṣṇava. The development of Nāṭya is thus analogous to that which has taken place in painting and poetry.

It may be remarked here that it is very usual for Indian singers, other than dancers, to accompany their singing with gesticulation. This is of two kinds, of which the first, quite distinct from what is spoken of in the present treatise, is a hand movement reflecting the musical form; this expression of empathy (*sādhāraṇī*) is sometimes very impressive or graceful, but not less often grotesque. The second, known as *bhāv batānā* or 'shewing moods' is of the type here described as *abhinaya*, or 'gesture' and differs from Nāṭya only in the greater relative importance of the music and the words.

Certain of the dance poses possess not merely a general linguistic, but also a special hieratic significance. These poses, chiefly of the hands, are spoken of as *mudrās* (seals), and are more or less familiar to students of Hindū iconography. It is, however, scarcely realised how closely connected are the dancing and the sculpture. Many of the gods are themselves dancers, and, in particular, the everlasting operation of creation, continuance, and destruction—the Eternal Becoming, informed by All-pervading Energy—is marvellously represented in the dance of Śiva.[1] He also exhibits dances of triumph and of destruction. Kālī, likewise, dances in the burning ground, which we understand to signify the heart of the devotee made empty by renunciation. Śrī Krishna dances a dance of triumph following the victory over

[1] "In this drama of the world He is both the Chief Actor and the Chief of Actresses. This drama commenced in the beginning with the union of Actor and Actress, and will conclude, according to His unfailing will, at that night which is the end of time" ("Tantra Tattva", trans. Avalon, p. 28).

Kāliya, and another General Dance, with the milkmaids of Brindāban, who are the souls of men.

Most of the dances just mentioned, however, except the Rāsa Maṇḍala or General Dance last spoken of, are Tāṇḍava dances and represent a direct cosmic activity. Those of the Nṛtya class, which set forth in narrative fashion the activities of Gods and Titans, or exhibit the relationships of hero and heroine " so as to reveal an esoteric meaning", are for the most part Lāsya dances performed by the Apsarās of Indra's paradise, and by the Devadāsīs and Nācnīs upon earth. It will be seen that in all cases the dance is felt to fulfil a higher end than that of mere entertainment: it is ethically justified upon the ground that it subserves the Four Ends of life, and this view of Nāṭya is plainly stated in Tiruvenkaṭācāri's preface translated below. The arts are not for our instruction, but for our delight, and this delight is something more than pleasure, it is the godlike ecstasy of liberation from the restless activity of the mind and the senses, which are the veils of all reality, transparent only when we are at peace with ourselves. From the love of many things we are led to the experience of Union: and for this reason Tiruvenkaṭācāri does not hesitate to compare the actor's or dancer's art with the practice of Yoga. The secret of all art is self-forgetfulness.

Side by side with this view, however, there has always existed in India a puritanical disparagement of the theatre, based upon a hedonistic conception of the nature of aesthetic emotion; and this party being now in full cry, and the Nautch, on the other hand, being threatened by that hybridization which affects all the arts of India that are touched by western influence, the old Indian Nāṭya is not likely to survive for very much longer. Probably the art of the theatre will now first be revived in Europe, rather than in India.

All that is said in the present volume will serve only as an introduction to Indian dramatic technique and to Oriental acting in general. But we are encouraged to think that even so brief an introduction to an extensive science may prove of practical value to the many dramatists who are interested in the future of the European theatre; and though we have done all in our power to serve the ends of scholarship, our main purpose in publishing the " Mirror of Gesture " is to interest and assist the living actor — not that we suppose that it might be profitable for him to adopt the actual gesture-language of the East, but that it may inspire him with the enthusiasm and the patience needful for the re-creation of the drama in his own environment.

It remains to be said that our translation is based upon a Nāgarī transcript of the second Telugu edition of the "Abhinaya Darpaṇa" of Nandikeśvara, published under the editorship of the late Tiruvenkaṭācāri of Niḍāmangalam. The translation is intended to be literal, but in the latter part, and occasionally elsewhere, is somewhat compressed by the omission of words that are not absolutely essential, or phrases that are constantly repeated, such as 'in the dance', 'this hand is called', or 'it is stated in the laws of dancing'.

My thanks are due to M. Victor Goloubew for the photographs reproduced on Plates I and III, while the illustrations on Plates IV and V (above) are from photographs by the Archaeological Survey of India.

ANANDA COOMARASWAMY

# THE INDIAN EDITOR'S PREFACE

The Bharata Śāstra, which is most dear to the Lord of Śrī, the Creator of every world, and which is the delight of every connoisseur in every world, has been brought into being by Śiva, Śambhu, Gaurī, Brahmā, Mādhava, Nandikeśvara, Dattila, Kohala, Yājñavalkya, Nārada, Hanuman, Vighrarāja, Subrahmaṇiya, Arjuna, and the daughter of Bāṇa (i. e. Uṣā): these are the famous authors of our science. Notwithstanding this, it is known to everyone that in these days our people not merely neglect this lore as though it were of the common sort, but go so far as to declare it to be an art that is only suited for the entertainment of the vulgar, unworthy of cultivated men, and fit to be practised only by play-actors. But it is like the Union-science (*Yoga-śāstra*) which is the means of attaining spiritual freedom (*mokṣa*): and the reason why a science such as this has come to be regarded in such a fashion is that it is by movements of the body (*angikābhinaya*) that the lineaments and interplay of hero and heroine, etc., are clearly exhibited, so as to direct men in the way of righteousness, and to reveal an esoteric meaning; obtaining the appreciation of connoisseurs and those who are learned in the lore of gesture. But if we understand this science with finer insight, it will be evident that it has come into being to set forth the sport and pastime of Śrī Krishna, who is the progenitor of every world, and the patron deity of the flavour of love; that by clearly expressing the flavour, and enabling men to taste thereof, it gives them the wisdom of Brahma, whereby they may understand how every business is unstable; from which understanding arises indifference (*vairāgya*) to such business, and therefrom arise the highest virtues of peace and patience, and thence again may be won the Bliss of Brahma.

It has been declared by Brahmā and others that the mutual relations of hero and heroine, in their esoteric meaning, partake of the nature of the relations of master and pupil, mutual service and mutual understanding; and therefore this Bharata Śāstra, which is a means to the achievement of the Four Aims of Human Life, — Virtue, Wealth, Pleasure, and Spiritual Freedom, — and the most exalted science, practised even by the Devas, should also be patronized and practised by ourselves.

So thinking, I resolved to restore the science to its former eminence, which has been day by day obscured. First of all was published the "Mirror of Gesture", composed by one of the founders of the science, Nandikeśvara, to wit; but as it was not readily understandable by all, there have been introduced into this second edition pictures of the "Hands", with descriptions, and also particulars of the occasion of their origin, race, patron deities, etc., mentioned in various works; and also combined hands, hands to indicate famous emperors, sacred rivers, trees; animals, such as the lion; birds, such as the swan; water-creatures, such as the crocodile; and a classification of "Heads." In this way a total of four hundred and eight new verses have been introduced, and therewith a simple translation with easy Telugu words such as women and children can understand.

Besides this we have published another book, the *Bhārata Rasa Prakaraṇa*, in which the Nine Flavours are explained, with Telugu translations; and there exists a reference work of the nature of a commentary, written by Rāja Mannāru Guḍi Sabhāpataya Gāru, containing full explanations of such technical terms as *rāga*, *tāla*, *nāyaka*, *nāyakā*, *rasa*, etc. May those of the public who are connoisseurs both patronize and give us their encouragement.

MAḌĀBHŪSHI TIRUVENKAṬA, OF NIḌĀMANGALAM,
A.D. 1887.

OṂ

MAY ALL BE WELL!

HAIL TO THE HOLY HAYAGRĪVA!

# THE MIRROR OF GESTURE

## DECLARED BY NANDIKEŚVARA

The movement of whose body is the world, whose speech the sum of all language,
Whose jewels are the moon and stars — to that pure Śiva I bow![1]

*Indra.* — I bow to Nandikeśvara, who dwells on Kailāsa's mount, the ocean of the essence of compassion, who reveals the meaning of the Laws of Dancing.

*Nandikeśvara.* — Welcome to the King of the Suras! Is it well with the dwellers in heaven? What is the cause that brings you here before me?

*Indra.* — This devotee of thine, this dancer, head of the dancing-hall thy patronage adorns, has come to ask a favour.

*Nandikeśvara.* — Tell me truly and fully what I can do for you.

*Indra.* — In the dancing-hall of the Daityas there is a dancer of the name of Naṭaśekhara. Indra seeks the Bharatārṇava, composed by thee, that he may gain the victory over him by authentic knowledge of the skill of dancing.

*Nandikeśvara.* — Hear, then, with attention the Bharatārṇava lore complete in four thousand verses.

*Indra.* — O Nandikeśvara, image of compassion, apart from that immensity, pray relate to me the authentic and entire Laws of Dancing in a more concise form.

*Nandikeśvara.* — O wise of heart, O Deva, I reveal accordingly an abridgment of the Bharatārṇava. Receive this simple "Mirror" attentively.

[1] In this verse Śiva is compared to an actor, whose means of expression (*abhinaya*) are gesture, voice, and costume. He reveals himself through the world, the speech of men, and the starry firmament. The image of Śiva as dancer (Naṭarāja, Naṭeśa) and actor is everywhere conspicuous in Śaiva literature (see "The Dance of Śiva", by A. K. Coomaraswamy, "Siddhānta Dīpika", Vol. XIII, i).

The sages speak of Nāṭya, Nṛtta, and Nṛtya.[1] Nāṭya is dancing used in a drama (*nāṭaka*) combined with the original plot. Nṛtta is that form of dance which is void of flavour (*rasa*) and mood (*bhāva*). Nṛtya is that form of dance which possesses flavour, mood, and suggestion (*rasa*, *bhāva*, *vyañjanā* etc.), and the like. There is a twofold division of these three, Lāsya and Tāṇḍava. Lāsya dancing is very sweet, Tāṇḍava dancing is violent.

Nāṭya and Nṛtya should be seen especially at festivals. Nṛtya at coronations, celebrations, processions of men or gods, marriages, reunion of friends, entry into towns or houses, the birth of children, and all auspicious occasions, by those who desire fortune. Brahmā has derived instrumental music, gesture, song, and flavour respectively from the Ṛg, Yajur, Sāma, and Atharva Vedas, and has made these Laws of Dancing which yield fulfilment of the Four Ends of Life, and are means to overcome misfortune, hurt, affliction, disappointment, and regret, and yield therewith more delight than even Brahma-bliss. Nṛtya should be seen by a royal audience in the courts of kings.

*The Audience* (sabhā). — The Audience shines like the Wishing-tree, when the Vedas are its branches, scriptures of art and science (*śāstras*) its flowers, and learned men the bees; where men of truth are found, shining with good qualities, famous for righteous conduct, honoured by kings, adorned by the Vedas; where the Vedānta is expounded; when distinguished by the sound of voice and lute (*vīṇā*); possessing heroes of renown, ornamented by resplendent princes, shining with royal splendour.

The Seven Limbs of the Audience are men of learning, poets, elders, singers, buffoons, and those who are familiar with history and mythology.

[1] Nṛtta and Nṛtya constitute dancing as a separate art. The ordinary performance of a *nācnī* (nautch-girl, *bayadère*) consists of alternate Nṛtya and Nṛtta, the former consisting of set dances with some special subject, and accompanied by varied gesture, the latter merely moving to and fro, marking time with the feet, and so forth. Nṛtta is here dismissed with a merely negative definition, as the object of the Abhinaya Darpaṇa is to explain how to express by gesture definite themes.

According to Dhanaṃjaya ("Daśarūpa" I, 14) speaking of Nṛtya and Nṛtta, "the former, gesture-with-meaning is high (*mārga*), the latter popular (*deśī*)."

*The Chief of the Audience* (sabhā-nāyaka). — He who is Chief of the Audience should be wealthy, wise, discriminating, full of gifts, versed in musical lore, omniscient, renowned, of charming presence, knowing the moods (*bhāvas*) [1] and their expression (*hāva*), void of jealousy and like faults, familiar with customary etiquette, sympathetic, a Dhīrodātta Nāyaka, expert in all the arts, clever in statecraft.

*The Ministers* (mantri). — Those who shine as royal ministers are men of their word, discerners of good qualities, wealthy, famed, learned in mood (*bhāva*), knowing good from evil, fain of the flavour of love, impartial, well-conducted, of good will, learned, devoted servants of the king, and men of culture.

*The Stage* (ranga). — The Chief of the Audience, as described, should sit at ease, facing the east, the poets, ministers, and courtiers at his side. The place before him, where dancing is to be done, is called the stage.

The danseuse (*pātra*) should stand in the middle of the stage, and the dancer (*naṭa*) near her; on the right the cymbalist (*tāladhārī*); on either side the drummers (*mṛdangikaḥ*); the chorus (*gītakāraḥ*) between them; and the drone (*śrūtikāra*) a little behind. Each of these, and thus ordered, should be present on the stage.

*The Danseuse, or Actress* (pātra). — It is understood that the Danseuse (*nartakī*) should be very lovely, young, with full round

[1] *Bhāva* is the first touch of emotion in a mind previously at rest; when the emotion becomes more intense, and finds expression in movements of the eyes, eyebrows, etc., it is called *hāva*. The ten *hāvas* or *sṛngāra-ceṣṭās* are included among the twenty or twenty-eight ornaments (*alankāra*) of a heroine, as follows: *līlā*, the imitation of the lover; *vilāsa*, a flutter of delight, *vicchitti*, rearrangement of dress or jewels to enhance loveliness; *vibhrama*, confusion or flurry; *kilakiñcita*, a combination of anger, tears, joy, fear, etc.; *moṭṭayita*, absorption in thoughts of the lover when his name is heard; *kuṭṭamita*, feigned anger; *bibboka*, feigned indifference; *lalita*, graceful swaying or lolling; *vihṛta*, silence imposed by modesty.

These are described in the "Sāhitya Darpaṇa" of Viśvanātha, "Dāśarūpa" of Dhanaṃjaya, "Bhāsa-bhuṣana" of Lāla-candrika, etc. The physical signs expressing the *hāvas* are detailed in subsequent verses of the "Mirror of Gesture," (e.g. pp. 20, 25). Strictly speaking, *bhāva* is mood or feeling unexpressed, *hāva* is the emotion which finds expression, *ceṣṭā* the gesture that expresses it. *Rasa* or flavour and *vyañjanā* or suggestion (transcending the literal meaning) distinguish poetry from prose.

breasts, self-confident, charming, agreeable, dexterous in handling the critical passages,[1] skilled in steps and rhythms, quite at home on the stage, expert in posing hands and body, graceful in gesture, with wide-open eyes, able to follow song and instruments and rhythm, adorned with costly jewels, with a charming lotus-face, neither very stout nor very thin, nor very tall nor very short.

*Disqualifications of a Danseuse.* — The Danseuse (*veśya*) should be rejected, whose eyes are (pale) like a flower, whose hair is scanty, whose lips are thick, or breasts pendant, who is very stout or very thin, or very tall or very short, who is humpbacked, or has not a good voice.

*The Bells* (kinkinī). — The Bells should be made of bronze or copper or silver; they should be sweet-toned, well-shaped, dainty, with the asterisms for their presiding deities, tied with an indigo string, with a knot between each pair of bells. At the time of dancing there should be a hundred or two hundred for each foot, or a hundred for the right foot and two hundred for the left.[2]

*The Dancer or Actor* (naṭa). — Wise men say the Dancer (or actor) should be handsome, of sweet speech, learned, capable, eloquent, of good birth, learned in the scriptures (*śāstras*) of art and science, of sweet voice, versed in song, instrumental music, and dancing, self-confident, and of ready wit.

*Outer Life* (bahiḥ prāṇa) *of the Danseuse.* — The following accessories are called the Outer Life of the Danseuse: the drum, cymbals of a good tone, the flute, the chorus, the drone, the lute (*vīṇā*), the bells, and a male singer (*gāyaka*) of renown.

*Inner Life* (antaḥ prāṇa) *of the Danseuse.* — The ten factors of the Inner Life of the Danseuse are swiftness, composure,

[1] *Kuśala graha-mokṣayoh,* lit. expert in grasping and releasing, emphasizing and relaxing the stress of emotion. The actress is not to be swayed by impulse, but perfectly self-possessed, mistress of a studied art, in accordance with the Telugu saying *bommale-vale ādintsuta*, "as if pulling the strings of a puppet", a phrase also used in speaking of the relation of God to man and the universe.

[2] No dancer ties the bells upon her ankles before dancing, without first touching her forehead and eyes with them, and repeating a brief prayer. Investiture with the bells makes the adoption of a professional life inevitable.

symmetry, versatility, glances, ease, intelligence, confidence, speech, and song.

*Vulgar Dancing* (nīca nāṭya). — Those who are versed in the Science of Dancing say that that dancing is vulgar in which the actress does not begin with prayer, etc.

*The Fruit of Witnessing Vulgar Dances.* — Those who look upon the dancing of such a vulgar actress will have no children, and will be reborn in animal wombs.

*The Course of the Dance* (nāṭya-krama). — What is said traditionally by our ancestors must therefore be kept in view. Having made the prayer, etc., the dancing may begin. The song should be sustained in the throat; its meaning must be shown by the hands; the mood (*bhāva*) must be shown by the glances; rhythm (*tāla*) is marked by the feet. For wherever the hand moves, there the glances follow; where the glances go, the mind follows; where the mind goes, the mood follows; where the mood goes, there is the flavour (*rasa*).

## GESTURE (*abhinaya*)

Gesture is the principal theme of what is here related.

The root *ni* with the prefix *abhi* implies exposition, and the word *abhinaya* is used in this sense. According to another book (*granthāntare*), *abhinaya* is so called because it evokes flavour (*rasa*) in the audience. There are three kinds of gesture:[1] bodily, vocal, and ornamental (*āngika*, *vācika*, *āhārya*), besides the pure, passionate, and dark (*sāttvika*, etc.). Here we are only concerned with *angikābhinaya*, "Exposition by means of the gestures of the body and limbs."

The three elements of bodily gesture are the limbs, parts of the body, and features (*anga*, *pratyanga*, *upānga*).

In *Angābhinaya* the head, hands, arm-pits, sides, waist, and feet, these six, and some say also the neck, are called the limbs.

[1] Observe that *abhinaya* strictly speaking means "expression" whether by gesture, singing, or costume. In the present work it is expression by gesture which is considered, and on this account the term *abhinaya* has been rendered by "gesture" throughout.

In *Pratyangābhinaya* the shoulders, shoulder-blades, arms, back, stomach, thighs and calves, some say also three others, the wrists, knees, and elbows, are the parts of the body.

In *Upāngābhinaya* the eyes, eyelids, pupils, cheeks, nose, jaw, the lips, teeth, tongue, chin, face, these eleven are the features. Beside these are the accessories, such as the heel, ankle, fingers and toes, and palms, which I mention according to the old books.

Only such as are useful in dancing will be described. The classification of Heads will be given first, then that of the Glances, Neck, Hands, and Actions, and from these five will appear the resulting movements.

*Nine Movements of the Head.* — The following nine Heads are named by those who are versed in the Science of Dancing: Sama, Udvāhita, Adhomukha, Ālolita, Dhuta, Kampita, Parāvṛtta, Utkṣipta, Parivāhita.

*Sama* (level): not moving, not bent, nor raised. Usage: at the beginning of dancing, prayer,[1] authoritative speech, satisfaction, anger, indifference, or inaction.

*Udvāhita* (raised): raising the head and keeping it still. Usage: flag, moon, firmament, mountain, flying things in the air, anything tall.

*Adhomukha* (face inclined): the head is bent. Usage: modesty, sorrow, bowing, regarding anything vile, fainting, things on the ground, bathing.

*Ālolita* (rolling): the head is moved in a circle. Usage: sleepiness, obsession, intoxication, faintness, dizziness, hesitation, laughter, etc.

*Dhuta* (shaken): the head is turned to and fro from right to left and left to right. Usage: denial, looking repeatedy at things, condolence with others, astonishment, dismay, indifference, cold, fire, fear, first moment of drinking liquor, preparing for battle, rejection, impatience, glancing at one's own limbs, summoning from both sides.

*Kampita* (nodded): shaking the head up and down. Usage: indignation, saying "Halt!", enquiry, summoning, threatening, etc.

[1] Cf. usage in "Bhagavad Gītā", VI, 13.

*Parāvṛtta* (turned round): the head is turned aside. Usage: saying "Do this", aversion, modesty, quiver, relaxing the features, slighting, hair, etc.

*Utkṣipta* (tossed): turning the head aside and upwards. Usage: saying "Take this", etc., indication, cherishing, assent.

*Parivāhita* (wagging): the head is moved from side to side like a fan. Usage: being in love, yearning for the beloved, pleasure, gratification, reflection (*vicāra*).

The twenty-four Heads following are mentioned elsewhere, by Bharatācārya and others: Dhuta, Vidhuta, Ādhuta, Avadhuta, Kampita, Akampita, Udvāhita, Parivāhita, Añcita, Nihañcita, Parāvṛtta, Utkṣipta, Adhomukha, Lolita, Tiryonnatānnata, Skandhānata, Ārātrika, Sama, Pārśvābhimukha, Saumya, Ālolita, Tirascīna, Prakampita, Saundarya.

*Dhuta:* moving the head slowly and regularly to and fro. Usage: an empty place, looking to one side, failing to find sympathy, astonishment, dismay, indifference, rejection.

*Vidhuta:* the same head, moved quickly. Usage: cold, heat, fear, the first moment of drinking liquor.

*Ādhuta:* slightly raising and turning the head sharply. Usage: everything, looking at one's own body, looking at the sides with an upward glance, ability to perform an action, dignity.

*Avadhuta:* inclining the head sharply. Usage: saying "Stay", pointing out a place, asking a question, summoning, conversation.

*Kampita:* raising the head high and shaking it. Usage: recognition, indignation, consideration (*vitarka*), threatening, hastening, questioning.

*Akampita:* the same movement slowly. Usage: something in front, enquiry, instruction (*upadeśa*), one's own opinion, narration.

*Udvāhita:* raising the head sharply. Usage: saying "I can", dignity.

*Parivāhita:* turning the head in a circle. Usage: shamelessness, misapprehension, keeping silence, recalling (the appearance etc. of) the beloved, astonishment, smiling, joy, horripilation, giving pleasure, reflection.

*Añcita* (bent): the neck is slightly bent to one side. Usage: regarding anything vile, being in love, fainting, etc., gazing at the middle of the lower lip.

*Nihañcita:* raising the shoulder, and touching it with the head. Usage: pleasure at seeing the beloved (*vilāsa*), graceful posing (*lalita*), affected indifference (*bibboka*), hysterics (*kilakiñcita*), rapture at being reminded of an absent lover (*moṭṭayita*), feigned anger (*kuṭṭamita*), modest silence (*mauna*), affectation of being unmoved (*stambha*).

*Parāvṛtta:* the head is averted. Usage: saying "Do this", aversion, modesty, etc., relaxing the features, following one who has gone aside, looking back.

*Utkṣipta:* the face is uplifted. Usage: things moving in the sky.

*Adhomukha:* the head is bent. Usage: modesty, sorrow, bowing.

*Lolita:* the head unsteady, the eyes languid as if from excess of pride. Usage: sleepiness, obsession, intoxication, faintness.

*Tiryonnatānnata:* the head is moved up and down. Usage: affected indifference.

*Skandhānata:* the head is rested on the shoulder. Usage: sleep, intoxication, fainting, anxiety (*cintā*).

*Ārātrika:* turning the head to both sides, just touching the shoulders. Usage: astonishment, inferring the opinions of others.

*Sama:* natural pose of the head. Usage: expressing normal circumstances.

*Pārśvābhimukha:* the head is turned aside in looking at persons on one side.

*Saumya:* motionless. Usage: when the dance (*nṛtya*) is to be begun.

*Ālolita:* the head is moved about freely. Usage: when flowers are offered in the hands, in Cārī-naṭana, charm (*lavana*).

*Tirascīna:* looking up on both sides. Usage: in dances showing modesty, and that called Mukhacārī, and such suitable occasions.

*Prakampita* (waving about): repeatedly moving the head forward and to both sides. Usage: the marvellous (*adbhuta rasa*), song, composition (*prabandha*), bee, the enemy's mode of fighting.

*Saundarya* (elegance): looking up and down, the trunk also bent. Usage: expressing a cause (*kāraṇa*), in dances showing the " bee " hand, yoga-practice.

*The Eight Glances* (aṣṭa dṛṣṭi).—In Bharataśāstra the following eight sorts of Eye or Glance (*dṛṣṭi*) are mentioned: Sama, Ālokita, Sāci, Pralokita, Nimīlita, Ullokita, Anuvṛtta, Avalokita.

*Sama* (level): gazing without winking, like a woman of the gods. Usage: beginning a dance, scales, thinking of some other matter, surprise, the image of a god.

*Ālokita* (inspecting): swiftly turning with keen glances. Usage: potter's wheel turning, showing "all sorts of things", desires.

*Sāci* (sidelong): looking out of the corners of the eyes, without moving the head. Usage: secret purpose (*ingita*), twirling the moustache (self-confidence), aiming an arrow, hinting, and in Kulaṭa nāṭya.

*Pralokita:* turning from side to side. Usage: looking at things on both sides, making signs, moving, disordered mind.

*Nimīlita* (closed): the eyes half-closed, half-open. Usage: appearance of a sage (*ṛṣi*), subjection to another's will, prayer (*japa*), meditation (*dhyāna*), greeting (*namaskṛta*), madness, keen insight (*sukṣma dṛṣṭi*).

*Ullokita* (looking up): directing the glance keenly up and aside. Usage: the point of a flag, tower (*gopura*), temple (*deva mandapa*), previous lives, height, moonlight.

*Anuvṛtta* (following): glancing quickly up and down. Usage: angry looks, friendly invitation.

*Avalokita* (looking down): looking down. Usage: looking at a shadow, reflection (*vicāra*), bed, study, looking at one's own body.

The following Glances are mentioned elsewhere: Sama, Pralokita, Snigdha, Srngara, Ullokita, Adbhuta, Karuṇa, Viṣmaya,

Tṛpta, Viṣanna, Bhayānaka, Sāci, Dṛta, Vīra, Raudra, Dūra, Ingita, Vilokita, Vitarkita, Śankita, Abhitapta, Avalokita, Śūnya, Hṛṣṭa, Ugra, Vibhrānta, Śānta, Mīlita, Sūcana, Lajjita, Malina, Trasta, Mlāna, Mukula, Kuñcita, Ākāśa, Ardhamukula, Anuvṛtta, Vipluta, Jihma, Vikośa, Madira, Hṛdaya, Lalita.

*Sama:* looks like those of the women of the gods (not winking, etc.). Usage: normal circumstances.

*Pralokita:* casting glances on both sides. Usage: looking on both sides.

*Snigdha* (tender): the look that is associated with joy, pleasant anticipation, things after one's own heart, having an inner radiance, expressing the surge of love passion. Usage: in affection.

*Sṛngāra* (love): born of great joy, in the toils of love — raising the eyebrows and looking out of the corners of the eyes. Usage: mutual glances of those who are fast bound by amorous desires.

*Ullokita:* looking upwards. Usage: tall things, previous births.

*Adbhuta:* the ends of the eyelids slightly curved, the eyebrows raised in wonder, the eyes shining. Usage: the marvellous.

*Karuṇa:* a downcast glance, half-vouchsafed, with tears, benevolent, the black pupil slowly moving, regarding the tip of the nose. Usage: the pathetic.

*Viṣmaya* (astonishment): quickly raised, straight-staring. Usage: astonishment.

*Tṛpta* (satisfaction): steady, wide-opened, the pupil motionless, keeping its place. Usage: resolution (*utsāha*).

*Viṣaṇṇa:* the eyelids wide apart, eyelashes recurved, the pupil fixed. Usage: dismay, anxiety.

*Bhayānaka* (inspiring fear): the eyelids raised and fixed, the pupil bright and fluttering. Usage: great fear, the terrible.

*Sāci:* looking persistently out of the corners of the eye. Usage: secret purpose.

*Dṛta* (fish ?): both pupils moving. Usage: excitement.

*Vīra* (heroic): radiant, direct, open, rather majestic, self-controlled, the pupils at rest. Usage: the heroic.

*Raudra* (cruel): unfriendly, red, cruel, the pupils fixed and the lids not moved, the brows contracted and raised. Usage: the cruel.

*Dūra* (far): slightly raised. Usage: things at a distance.

*Ingita:* sidelong glances expressing joy. Usage: secret thought.

*Vilokita:* looking back. Usage: things or places behind.

*Vitarkita* (deliberation): direct, wide-opened, the eyelids separated, the pupils fixed as if in fear. Usage: consideration (*ūhā*).

*Śankita* (apprehensive): a little moved, a little at rest, slightly raised and moved to and fro, the pupils partly hidden. Usage: hesitation.

*Abhitapta* (burnt): the eyelids moving, the pupils gazing languidly. Usage: indifference (i. e. regarding a thing, but without interest).

*Avalokita:* looking down. Usage: study (*paṭhanā*), reflection (*vicāra*).

*Śūnya* (vacant): eyelids level, pupils visible, motionless, gaze vacant. Usage: misunderstanding (*bāhyārtha grahaṇa*).

*Hṛṣṭa* (merry): fluttering, pleasant, twinkling. Usage: laughter.

*Ugra* (fierce): very wide open, a little red at the corners. Usage: ferocity.

*Vibhrānta* (wandering): the pupils moving, rolling, unconstrained, between tears and laughter; the wandering glance of excitement.

*Śānta* (peace): gradually closing the lids, the eyes slightly moving, the pupils moving to the corners; the peaceful glance of dispassion.

*Mīlita*: nearly closed. Usage: conditions such as subjection to another's will.

*Sūcana:* the eyes partly closed, following the movement of the (*sūci*) hand. Usage: pointing out.

*Lajjita:* the upper eyelid dropped, the pupil also lowered bashfully, the lashes meeting; this modest glance is used modestly.

*Malina:* the lashes partly closed as if by rheum, the pupils sunken; this unclean eye denotes women (i. e. dissipation).

*Trasta* (frightened): inwardly expanded, the pupil raised. Usage: fear and intoxication.

*Mlāna* (dull): the pupils moving languidly and slowly, squinting, the lashes seeming to touch; this dull eye indicates insipid matters.

*Mukula:* the lashes trembling and touching, the expression of the pupils mild, the upper lids lowered; this 'bud' eye indicates bliss (*ānanda*).

*Kuñcita* (curved): the lashes a little recurved, the eyeballs a little sunk; dislike, or jealousy.

*Ākāśa* (sky): directed towards the sky, the pupil turned far back; indicating things moving above.

*Ardhamukula:* smiling, the pupils just visible under the lids; this 'half-bud' eye indicates bliss and rejoicing.

*Anuvṛtta* (following): repeated glancing; it is used in hurry.

*Vipluta:* the lids trembling, expanded, and then dropped; this 'disordered' eye indicates beauty in things of all sorts.

*Jihma* (oblique): bent back, a slow and hidden glance; used to convey secret meanings, and in envy.

*Vikośa:* without winking, the pupils moving, the lids wide apart; it is used in joy.

*Madira:* indirect, ranging, centred, unsteady, crooked; it is used to indicate the early stage of intoxication.

*Hṛdaya:* unsteady, flurried, the pupils moving somewhat (*anaglulita*), the lids recurved; it is used for mediocre things.

*Lalita* (graceful): the corners of the eyes closed by the movement of the brows, smiling because of the working of Love, direct; it is used in graceful posing (*lalita*), etc.

According to another book there are named the following six movements of the Brows: Sahaja, Patita, Utkṣipta, Catura, Recita, Kuñcita.

*Sahaja:* the natural brow in a smooth face. It expresses the natural state.

*Patita:* the brows being at rest, are made to frown. Usage: distaste, astonishment, jealousy.

*Utkṣipta:* either one or both of the brows is raised. Usage: woman's anger, telling the truth, feelings of love (*sṛngāra-bhāva*), dalliance (*līlā*).

*Catura:* the brows meeting and faintly quivering. It is used in touching one another's face, heart's bliss, and excitement.

*Recita:* one brow is contracted with charm and sweetness. Usage: listening to a secret, saying "Sādhu", looking at any place.

*Kuñcita:* one or both brows arched. Usage: rapture at being reminded of an absent lover (*moṭṭayita*), feigned anger (*kuṭṭa-mita*), pleasure at seeing the beloved (*vilāsa*), hysterics (*kila-kiñcita*).

Knowers of mood (*bhāva*) have declared that there are four Necks: Sundari, Tirascīna, Parivartita, Prakampita.

*Sundari:* moving to and fro horizontally (*tiryak pracalita*).[1] Usage: the beginning of affection, making trial, saying "Well done!", recollection, badinage, sympathetic pleasure.

*Tirascīna:* an upward movement on both sides, like the gliding of a snake. Usage: brandishing a sword, serpentine progression.

*Parivartita:* moving to right and left, like a half-moon. Usage: *Sṛṅgara naṭana* (erotic dances), when kissing the cheeks.

*Prakampita:* moving the head backwards and forwards like a pigeon. Usage: saying "You and I", especially in *Deśīya naṭa* (folk-dances), swings, counting.

*Lives of the Hands* (hasta prāṇa). — The Lives (i. e. movements) of the Hands are twelve, as follows: Prasāraṇa, Kuñcita, Recita, Punkhita, Apaveṣṭita, Prerita, Udveṣṭita, Vyāvṛtta, Parivṛtta, Sanketa, Cihna, Padārtha-ṭīka.[2]

[1] This is one of the most characteristic, and at the same time most peculiar, movements of Indian dancing.

[2] The above-mentioned technical terms are used in the subsequent detailed description of the hands and in more detailed texts such as those quoted on p. 12 of the Preface. Nos. 5 and 7 are produced by turning the forearm on its own axis, so that the palm of the hand faces downwards (No. 5) or upwards (No. 7). In No. 8 the fingers point vertically upwards: in No. 9 the fingers point across the body.

*Prasāraṇa* (outspread): extending the fingers (e.g. Plate X A).

*Kuñcita* (bent, inclined): bending the fingers (e.g. Plate XI A).

*Recita* (separated): separating the fingers (e.g. Plate XI C, E).

*Punkhita* (feathered, or fluttering): the hand (directed) forward, (the fingers being) extended, bent, or separated (e.g. Plate XII B). This movement is used in Patāka and other hands.

*Apaveṣṭita* (twisted down): the hand directed downwards (e.g. Plate I, foremost hand and Plate XIII C, l.h.).

*Prerita* (directed): the hand turned back, (the fingers being) extended, bent, or separated (e.g. Plate VII D, XII A).

*Udveṣṭita* (twisted upwards): the hand directed (palm) upwards (e.g. Plates XI E, XII C, XIII D.)

*Vyāvṛtta* (turned back): the hand pointing upwards sideways (e.g. Plate VIII).

*Parivṛtta* (turned round): the hand directed forwards, sideways.

*Sanketa* (intimation): communicating an idea without words.[1]

*Cihna* (mark): the various *Cihnas* are the marks of those things which are evident, and of those unseen, their state of movement or rest, and eight others, viz. their form, face, situation, banner, weapons, virtues, range, and habits, as set forth in dance.

*Padārtha-ṭīka* (word-meaning commentary): the meaning of words is conveyed.

*The Classification of Hands* (hasta bheda). — The characteristics of the Hands will be set forth in order. There are two kinds, the Single (*asamyutta*) and the combined (*samyutta*). There are twenty-eight Single Hands as follows: Patāka, Tripatāka, Ardha-patāka, Kartarī-mukha, Mayura, Ardha-candra, Arāla, Śuka-tuṇḍaka, Muṣṭi, Śikhara, Kapittha, Kaṭaka-mukha, Sūci, Candra-kalā, (Padma-) Kośa, Sarpa-śīrṣa, Mṛga-śīrṣa, Siṃha-mukha, Lāngula, Sola-padma, Catura, Bhramara, Haṃsāsya, Haṃsa-pakṣa, Saṃdaṃsa, Mukula, Tāmracūḍa, Triśūla.

*Patāka* (flag): the thumb bent to touch the fingers, and the fingers extended. Usage: beginning a dance, cloud, forest, forbidding things, bosom, night, river, world of the gods, horse,

[1] *Akṣara-muṣṭikā*, communicating letters or ideas by the disposition of the fingers, is one of the 'sixty-four arts.'

cutting, wind, reclining, walking, prowess, graciousness, moonlight, strong sunlight, knocking, meaning of the seven cases, wave, entering a street, equality, applying sandal paste, one's self, taking an oath, silence, benediction, a good king, palmyra leaf, slap, touching, saying "Such and such", the sea, the way of good deeds, addressing (a person some distance away), going in front, the form of a sword, month, year, rainy season, day, sprinkling water.

According to another book, the thumb is bent against the base of the forefinger and the palm and fingers extended. When Brahmā, the Shaper, went to Parabrahmā, as he saluted him with the cry of "Victory!" he held his hand like a flag, since when it has been called the "flag hand". It is the first of all hands, it originates from Brahmā, its colour is white, its sage Śiva, its race Brāhmaṇa, its patron deity Parabrahmā. Usage: saying "Victory, victory!", clouds, forbidding things, forest, night, saying "Go!", going, conveyance, wind, chest, front, merit (*puṇya*), preëminence, flow, abode of the wise, crying "Ha! ha!", moonlight, sunlight, abode of the gods, removal of hindrance, wall, cutting, pleasing others, cheek, applying sandal paste, mustering an army, boundary, removing fear,[1] having no refuge, decrease, covering, reclining, the earth, flame, pouring rain, wave, wings of a bird, petitioning a king, saying "Thus", eye, saying "Like what?" and "Like that", slap, touching, lake, massage, closing a dispute, strong wind, end of the robe (*añcala*), cold, heat, radiance, shadow, ear, season, half-year, day, fortnight, month, purity, high birth, approach, saying "Protect", or "Caress", Brāhmaṇa caste, pure colour. (Plate X A.).

*Tripatāka* (three parts of the flag): the third finger of the Patāka hand is bent. Usage: a crown, tree, *vajra* weapon, the bearer of the *vajra* (Indra), screw-pine flower, light, rising flames, cheek, patterns drawn on the face or body (*patralekhā*), arrow, turning round, union of woman and man.

[1] The *Patāka* hand is commonly seen in the *abhaya mudrā* of images, but is sometimes replaced by *ardha-candra*.

According to another book: same definition. It is so called since Śakra (Indra) and others held the *vajra* weapon with three parts of the "flag", leaving out the third finger. Its colour is red, it is of Kṣattriya race, its sage is Guha, its patron deity Śiva. Usage: invocation, descent (*avataraṇa*), lifting or bending down the face, touching auspicious things, hook, site (*khala*), disrespect, doubt, crown, tree, Vāsava (Indra), *vajra*, stroking the hair, lamp, marking the brow-spot, tying a turban, applying strong scents, closing the nose or ears, rubbing-down a horse, arrow, screw-pine flower, patterns drawn on the face or body, the flight of certain birds, tongues of flame, Kṣattriya caste, red colour.[1] (Plates VII B, XII A.)

*Ardha-patāka* (half-flag): the little finger of the Tripatāka hand is also bent. Usage: tender shoots (*pallava*), panel for writing or drawing (*phalaka*), bank of a river, dagger (*krakaca*), knife, flag, tower (*gopura*), horn (*sṛnga*), saying "Both."

*Kartarī-mukha* (arrow shaft face): in the same hand, the forefinger and little finger are outspread.[2] Usage: separation of woman and man, opposition or overturning, stealing, the corner of the eye, death, disagreement, lightning, sleeping alone, falling, a creeper.

According to another book: the forefinger of the Tripatāka hand is out(-spread). Once upon a time, the sages say, Śaśānka-śekhara (Śiva), set out to slay Jaḍandhara; he drew a circle round the centre of the earth with his forefinger, and that is the origin of the Kartarī-mukha hand. It originates from Śiva, its sage is Parjaniya, its race Kṣattriya, its colour coppery, its patron deity Cakrapāṇi (Vishnu). Usage: red paint for the feet (*padā-*

[1] According to Dhanaṃjaya ("Daśarūpa", I, 126) the Tripatāka hand is used in stage whispers (*janāntika*) to shut out the others when only one person is addressed out of several present on the stage, e. g. "Śakuntalā", vi, 24.

[2] A fuller description of the Kartarī-mukha hand is quoted by T. A. Gopinatha Rao, from an unnamed source, in "Hindu Iconography," 1914, p. xxxi, where it is stated that it is used for holding attributes (cf. on Plate XI c) such as the conch and discus; and also that the thumb and third finger should meet near the middle of the palms. The hands of images conform to this rule in most cases, but not invariably. Most likely there exists some confusion of Kartarī-mukha and Mayura hands. Our figure shows the Kartarī-mukha hand according to the text description.

*laktaka*), drawing patterns on the body, yearning of separated husband and wife, overturning or opposition, Mādhava, lightning, sleeping alone, buffalo, deer, fly-whisk, hill-top, elephant, bull, cow, thick coil of hair, Kṣattriya caste, copper colour, scissors, tower. (Plates VII D, XI C.)

*Mayura* (peacock): the third finger of the Kartarī-mukha hand is joined to the thumb, the other fingers extended. Usage: the peacock's beak, a creeper, bird of omen (*śakuna*), vomiting, forehead, stroking the hair, forehead, brow-spot, wiping away tears, argument according to law (*śāstra*), renown.

*Ardha-candra* (half-moon):[1] the thumb of the Patāka hand is stretched out. Usage: the moon on the eighth day of the dark fortnight, a hand seizing the throat, a spear, consecrating an image, a platter, origin, waist, anxiety, one's self, meditation, prayer, touching the limbs, greeting common people.

According to another book: same definition. This hand originates from the desire of Śiva for ornaments, of which the moon is one. Its sage is Atri, its race Vaiṣya, its colour smoky, its patron deity Mahādeva. Usage: bangle, wrist, mirror, astonishment, effort, intemperance, entirety, beating time, tying up the hair, supporting the cheek in grief, the ear of an elephant, expelling evil-doers, wiping sweat from the brow, adolescence, ability, moon, greeting common people, consecration, eyebrow, cloth, bow, preëminence, tightening the girdle, making a vessel, the body, movement of the feet, carrying a child, the back, white colour, Vaiṣya caste. (Plate X B.)

*Arāla* (bent): the first finger of the Patāka hand is curved. Usage: drinking poison, nectar, etc., or sharp acid.

According to another book: the thumb and forefinger of the Patāka hand are curved. It was first used by Agastya in drinking (*āpośanam kṛte*) the seven seas. Its colour is red, its race mixed, its patron deity Vāsudeva — such is its history according to Bharata and others. Usage: the sipping of water (*āpośana*)

[1] This hand often replaces the Patāka, e. g., in the Abhaya mudrā of Plates I,

by Brāhmaṇas, benediction, the aversion of a parasite (*viṭā*) for his friend, dressing the hair, saying " Come soon ! ", circumambulation at morning and evening prayer, wiping sweat from the brow, putting collyrium on the eyes, etc.

*Śukatuṇḍaka* (parrot's beak): the third finger of the Arāla hand is also bent. Usage: shooting an arrow, throwing a spear (*kunta*), mystery (*marma*), ferocity.

According to another book: same definition. It originates from Pārvatī, who used it in a lover's quarrel with Sadāśiva. Its sage is Dhruvasa, its race Brāhmaṇa, its colour red, its patron deity Mārici. Usage: Brahmā-weapon, nose (*mukhāgra*), curve, turning round, javelin, proceeding, fighting, crossing, disrespect, lovers' quarrel, opinion, abandonment, dice, throwing a spear, ferocity, secrecy, copper colour, Brāhmaṇa caste. (Plate X F.)

*Muṣṭi* (fist): the four fingers are bent into the palm, and the thumb set on them. Usage: steadiness, grasping the hair, holding things, wrestling.

According to another book: the thumb placed on the middle finger, and the fingers closed. It originates from Vishnu, who used this hand when he fought with Madhu. Its sage is Indra, colour indigo, race Śūdra, patron deity the moon. Usage: grasping, waist, fruit, agreement, saying "Very well", sacrificial offerings, greeting common people, carrying away, strong hold, holding a book, running, lightness, wrestling, holding a shield, holding the hair, fisticuffs, grasping a mace or spear, indigo colour, Śūdra caste. (Plate X C.)

*Śikhara* (spire): in the same hand, the thumb is raised. Usage: the God of Love (*Madan*), bow, pillar, silence, husband, tooth, entering, questioning, the body, saying " No ! ", recollection, intimate suggestion (*abhinayāntara*), untying the girdle, embrace, lover, letting fly *śakti* and *tomara* weapons, sound of a bell, pounding.

According to another book: same definition. It originates from Candraśekhara (Śiva), when he held Mt. Meru as his bow.

It originates from that Meru-bow, its sage is Jihna, its race Gandharva, its colour dusky, the God of Love (*Rati vallabha*) its patron deity. Usage: gratifying the ancestors, steadiness, establishing a family, hero, spire, friend, cleaning the teeth with to and fro movement, plying a palmyra fan, difference, saying "What?", drinking water from a spouted vessel (*bhṛngāra*), the number four, letting fly *śakti* or *tomara* weapons, enjoying consequences, demure attitude of an amorous girl, bashfulness, bow, the God of Love (*Smara*), saying "No!", charity, permanent mood (*sthayi bhāva*), Vināyaka, Mahiṣa-mardinī, heroism, galloping of a horse, half-moon, brow-spot, etc., making the sign of the hair-knot, sapphire, intensity. (Plates X D, XII D, XV C.)

*Kapittha* (elephant-apple): the forefinger of the Śikhara hand is bent over the top of the thumb. Usage: Lakṣmī, Sarasvatī, winding, holding cymbals, milking cows, collyrium, holding flowers at the time of dalliance, grasping the end of the robe (*celāñcala*), veiling the head with the *añcala*, offering incense or lights, etc.

According to another book: same definition. Long ago when the Churning of the Ocean was done, Vishnu used this hand to pull upon Mt. Mandara. Its sage is Nārada, its race Ṛṣi, its colour white, its patron deity Padmagarbha (Vishnu). Usage: churning, Lakṣmī, offering incense or lights, etc., spreading cowries, holding elephant goad or *vajra*, or a sling, or cymbals, showing a dance (*nāṭya*), holding a lotus of dalliance (*līlābja dhāraṇa*), counting Sarasvatī's rosary, pounding barley etc., seizing the end of the robe (*celāñcala*), Ṛṣi caste, white colour.

*Kaṭaka-mukha* (opening in a link): the forefinger and middle finger are applied to the thumb.[1] Usage: picking flowers,

[1] The tip of the forefinger and the side of the middle finger are applied to the tip of the thumb, the third finger is bent beside the middle finger, and the little finger is also bent, but to a less degree. According to T. A. Gopinatha Rao, "Hindu Iconography," Vol. I, pt. 1, description of terms, p. 16, this hand (syn. *Siṃha-karṇa*) in images is generally intended to receive the daily offering of a fresh flower, and this is supported by the Ajaṇṭā usage.

This hand is also used in teaching and is known to some iconographers, perhaps incorrectly, as *Vitarka mudrā*.

holding a pearl necklace or garland of flowers, drawing a bow slowly, distributing folded betel leaves, applying such things as musk or scent, speech, glancing.

According to another book: the thumb of the Kapittha hand is thrown forward. This hand originated when Guha received instruction in archery from Śiva. Its sage is Bhārgava, its colour coppery, its race Deva, its presiding deity Raghurāma. Usage: holding a pearl or flower garland or a fly-whisk, drawing out an arrow, holding out a mirror, reins, conveyance, breaking a twig, cleaning the teeth, picking flowers, distributing folded betel leaves, applying musk, embrace of harlots, drawing the bow, holding the discus, holding a fan, gold colour, Deva caste. (Plate XI A.)

*Sūci* (needle): the forefinger of the Kaṭaka-mukha hand is upraised. Usage: one, Parabrahmā, demonstration, one hundred, sun, city, world, saying "Thus", or "What?", "He", fan, threatening, pining away, rod, the body, astonishment, braid of hair, umbrella, capability, down (*roma*), beating the drum, turning the potter's wheel, wheel, circle, explanation, evening.

According to another book: same definition. It originates from Brahmā, when he said "I am unique." Its sage is the sun, its race Deva, its colour white, its patron deity Viśvakarmā. Usage: boastings, truth-telling, pointing to a distant country, life, going in front, one, the twilights, solitude, lotus stalk, saying "Sādhu", looking at things, saying "Thus", world, Parabrahmā, unity, rod, turning a wheel, sun, sunrise and sunset, arrow, secret, hero (*nāyaka*), *śilī-mukha* arrow, saying "What?", saying "He", metal, handle, threatening, addressing inferiors, listening, yearning for the beloved, recollection, nose, beak, white colour, vision. (Plate XIII A.)

*Candra-kalā* (digit of the moon): the thumb of the Sūci hand is released. Usage: to indicate the crescent moon (Plate XIV A).

*Padmakośa* (lotus bud): the fingers separated and a little bent, the palm a little hollowed. Usage: fruit, wood-apple, elephant-apple, etc., breast, curve, ball of flowers, light food, bud, mango, rain of flowers, cluster of flowers, the *japā*-flower, the shape of a bell, the hole of a snake, a water-lily, an egg.

According to another book: the hand is like a perfect white lotus. Nārāyaṇa used this hand when worshipping Śiva with lotus flowers to obtain the discus. Its sage is Padmadhara, its race Yakṣa, and it also partakes of the Kinnara kind, its presiding deity is Bhārgava. Usage: trunk of an elephant, brilliance, vessel of gold or silver, coil of hair, moderation, charm, saying "Sādhu", bell, ball of flowers, lotus, hole of a snake, etc., curve, breast, coconut, mango, *karṇikāra*, mirror, bending a bough, rain of flowers, pot, egg, opening (of a flower), wood-apple, elephant-apple. (Plate XI D.)

*Sarpa-śīrṣa* (snake-head): the middle of the Patāka hand is hollowed. Usage: sandal-paste, snake, slowness, sprinkling, cherishing, etc., giving water to gods and sages, the flapping of elephants' ears, massage of wrestlers.

According to another book: same definition. This hand is derived from Vishnu, who showed it when he offered to protect the Devas against Bali, and promised to put him down. Its sage is Vāsava (Indra), its colour turmeric, its race Deva, its patron deity Śiva. Usage: rouge (*kunkuma*), mud, *prāṇāyama*,[1] washing the face, occasion of charity, sandal paste, elephant, a short man, massage of wrestler's shoulders, fondling, milk, water, saffron, bashfulness, concealing a child, image, drinking water, clinging (*līna*), saying "Very true", Brāhmaṇa caste, turmeric colour, saying "It is proper", answering, sprinkling sandal powder, applying sandal paste, etc., holding the breasts, etc. of women.

*Mṛga-śīrṣa* (deer-head): in the above hand, the thumb and little finger are extended. Usage: women, cheek, traditional manners (*krama-maryāda*), fear, discussion, costume of an actor (*naipathya*), place of residence, tête-à-tête, drawing

[1] To indicate *prāṇāyama* the *sarpa śīrṣa* hand is held upon the bridge of the nose, precisely as in the daily ritual of regulated breathing.

three lines on the brow, patterns on the ground, massage of the feet, combining, house, holding an umbrella, stair, placing the feet, calling the beloved, roaming.

According to another book: the thumb and little finger are raised. It springs from Gaurī, who used the Mṛga-śīrsa hand to draw three lines on her forehead when practising *tapas* for the sake of Śiva. Its race is Ṛṣi, its sage is Mārkaṇḍeya, its colour white, its presiding deity Maheśvara. Usage: wall, deliberation, opportunity, place of residence, *Padminī*, *Śankhinī* or *Hastinī* woman, slowness, applying sandal paste etc., gestures (*abhinaya*) of women, screen, stair, self-manifestation, order, having three lines drawn on the brow, consideration (*vitarka*), deer-face, indicating one's self, the body, Ṛṣi caste, white colour.

*Siṃha-mukha* (lion-face): the tips of the middle and third fingers are applied to the thumb, the rest extended. Usage: coral, pearl, fragrance, stroking the hair, a drop of water, salvation (*mokṣa*) when placed on the heart, *homa*, hare, elephant, waving *kuśa* grass, lotus garland, lion-face, testing the preparation of medicine. (Plates XII B, XIII A.)

*Lāngula* (tail): the third finger of the Padmakośa hand is bent. Usage: *lakuca*-fruit, breast of a young girl, white water-lily (*kalhāra*), partridge, areca-nut, little bells, pill, *cātaka*.

According to another book: the thumb, middle and forefinger held like the eye of a coconut, the third finger bent, and the little finger erect. It is derived from Śiva when he made a pellet of the poison that sprang from the sea of milk. Its sage is Krauñca, its race Siddha, its colour golden, its patron deity Padma. Usage: grapes, *rudrākṣa* seeds, holding the chin, breast-bud (*kuca-praroha*), areca-nut, bells, blue lotus, fruit, coral, a mouthful, asterism (*nakṣatra*), jujube fruit, circle, partridge, *cātaka*, anything small, hailstone, Siddha caste, myrobalan fruit, gold.

*Sola-padma* (full-blown lotus) (= *Ala-padma*): all the fingers separated, turned about the little finger. Usage: full-blown lotus, elephant-apple etc., turning, breast, yearning for the beloved, mirror, full-moon, a beautiful vessel, hair-knot, moon-pavilion (*candra-śālā*), village, height, anger, lake, car, *cakravāka* (bird), murmuring sound, praise.

According to another book: it is the *Ala-pallava* hand when there is turning. It originates from Śrī Krishna, when he was stealing butter and milk. Its sage is Vasanta, its race Gandharva, its colour dusky, its patron deity the Sun. Usage: fresh *ghī*, yearning for the beloved, head, sweetmeat, full-blown lotus, cluster of flowers, crown, ball, praises, beauty of form, dancing (*narṭana*), fort, palace, braided hair, moon-pavilion, sweetness, saying " Sādhu ", palmyra fruit. (Plate XII c.)

*Catura*: the thumb is bent to touch the base of the third finger, the first and adjoining fingers outstretched together, and the little finger extended (separately). Usage: musk, a little, gold, copper etc., wet, sorrow, aesthetic emotion (*rasāsvāda*), eyes, difference of caste, oath, playful converse (*sarasa*), slow-stepping, breaking to pieces, seat (*āsana*), oil or *ghī*, etc.

According to another book: in the Patāka hand, the thumb is made to touch the middle line of the third finger, and the little finger is stretched out. It originates from Kaśyapa, who used this hand to show the way to Garuḍa when he wished to steal the nectar. Its sage is Valakhilya, its colour variegated, its race mixed, its patron deity Vainateya. Usage: *gorocana*, dust, playful converse, red paint (*laktaka*), concentration of mind (or attention), camphor, eye, chin, earring, face, brow, side glance, beloved, policy, musk, sugar, honey, oil, *ghī*, cleverness, mirror, gold, diamond, emerald, sufficiency, a little, a moderate quantity of anything, indigo, white colour, mixed caste, sword, cheek, tip of the ear.

*Bhramara* (bee): the second finger and thumb touching, the forefinger bent, the rest extended. Usage: bee, parrot, crane (*sārasa*), cuckoo (*kokila*), union (*yoga*).

According to another book: the forefinger of the Haṃsāsya hand is bent. It originates from Kaśyapa when he was making earrings for the mother of the Devas. Its sage is Kapila, its colour dark, its race Khacara, its patron deity the King of Flying Creatures (Garuḍa). Usage: union (*yoga*), vow of silence, horn, tusk of an elephant, picking flowers with long stalks, bee, uttering the *karṇa-mantra*, taking out a thorn, untying the girdle, adverbs of two letters, flying creatures, dark colour. (Plate X E.)

*Haṃsāsya* (swan-face): the middle and following fingers are separated and extended, the forefinger and thumb are joined. Usage: tying the marriage thread, initiation, certainty, horripilation, painting (*citra-samlekhana*), gad-fly, drop of water, raising the wick of a lamp, rubbing (metal on a touchstone), examining things, drawing lines, carrying garlands, signifying "Soham" (That am I), metaphor (*rūpaka*), saying "No!", indicating things to be examined by rubbing, accomplishment of a task.

According to another book: the tips of the forefinger, middle finger and thumb are joined, the rest extended. This hand is derived from Dakṣiṇa-mūrti (Śiva), when he was teaching the Tattva system to the sages at the foot of the Nyagrodha tree. Its sage is Śukha, its colour white, its race mixed, its presiding deity Caturānana (Brahmā). Usage: instructing in wisdom, ritual (*pūjā*), demonstration of a thesis (*nirṇaya*), offering sesamum, speaking, reading, singing, meditation (*dhyāna*), demonstrating *bhāva*, applying wax, horripilation, pearl, gem, sound of the flute, gathering together (*samyutta*), smell, own self, drop of water, taking aim, seal-ring, kissing, Brāhmaṇa caste, white colour. (Plate VII c.)

*Haṃsa-pakṣa* (swan-feather): the little finger of the Sarpa-śīrṣa hand is extended. Usage: the number six, constructing a bridge, making marks with the nails, arranging.

According to another book: same definition. It is said to be associated with *tāṇḍava* dancing, and springs from Tāṇḍi. Its sage is Bharata, its colour indigo, its race Apsara, its patron deity the God of Love (Pañcasāyaka). Usage: constructing a bridge, restraining, gathering, feathers of a bird, completion, drawing a portrait (*rūpa-lekhana*), dusky colour, Apsara caste, and in Śubha-nāṭya.

*Saṃdaṃsa* (grasping): the fingers of the Padmakośa hand are repeatedly opened and closed. Usage: generosity, sacrificial offerings, tumour, insect, apprehension, worship (*arcana*), the number five.

According to another book: the middle finger of the Haṃsāsya hand is outstretched.[1] This hand originates from the Goddess of Speech, when she bestowed a rosary. Its sage is Viśvavāsu, its race Vidhyādhara, its colour white, its patron deity Vālmīki. Usage: tooth, small bud, singing (*saṃgīta*), gentle dances (*lāsya-naṭana*), exegesis (*ṭīka*), *jñāna-mudrā*, scales, flaw in a tooth, sacred thread (*yajñopavīta*), line, examining, painting pictures (*citra lekhana*), truth, saying " No ! ", saying " A little ", moment, listening, testing metals etc. on the touchstone (*nikaṣa*), shining white, taking aim, nail, sprout, *gunja* seed, the number eight, fire-fly, poison, blades of grass, red ants, mosquito, eclipse, collecting pearls, bug, fly, garland, down, pointing (*sūcana*), solitude, touching, Veda, snow, speaking, slipping, cutting off, a wound, brow-spot, collyrium, Vidyādhara caste, white colour, slowness.

*Mukula* (bud): the thumb and fingers are brought together so as to show their tips. Usage: water-lily (*kumuda*), eating, the God of Love (*Pañcabāṇa*), holding a seal, navel, plaintain flower.

According to another book: the fingers of the Padmakośa hand are brought together. It originates from the Scion of the Wind (Hanuman) when he attempted to seize the sun, mistaking it for a ripe *bimba* fruit. Its sage is Viśākhila, its race Sankīrṇa, its colour tawny, its patron deity the Moon. Usage: charity (*dāna*), prayer (*japa*), humble speech, eating, lotus bud, self (*ātman*), life (*prāṇa*), the number five, behaviour of an amorous woman, kissing children, worshipping the gods, umbrella etc., bud, accepting fruits, mixed race, brown colour.

[1] In this case, exceptionally, the definition quoted " from other books " differs markedly from that of Nandikeśvara: this form of Saṃdaṃsa hand is identical with Nandikeśvara's Haṃsāsya hand, and is quite distinct in form and significance from his Saṃdaṃsa.

*Tāmra-cuḍa* (red-crest, i. e. cock): the forefinger of the Mukula hand is bent. Usage: cock etc., crane (*baka*), camel, calf, writing or drawing.

According to another text: the thumb and little finger of the Patāka hand are pressed together. Of old, when the Three Vedas assumed a visible form, and stood before Brahmā to make exposition of themselves, they used this hand. Its sage is Vajrāyudha (Indra), its colour mother of pearl, its race Deva, its patron deity Bṛhaspati. Usage: the Three Worlds, trident, the number three, wiping away tears, the Three Vedas, wood-apple leaf, rubbing down a horse, leaf, panel (*phalaka*), cock, Deva race, white colour.

*Triśūla* (trident): the thumb and little finger are bent. Usage: wood-apple leaf, three together.

Thus the Twenty-eight Hands are set forth. But it is said that there are as many hands as meanings.

According to another text (three others are mentioned, as follows):

*Urṇa-nābha* (spider): the fingers of the Padmakośa hand are bent. It originates from Narasiṃha when he was tearing the body of the Daitya (Hiraṇyakaśipu). Its sage is Sārdulaka, its race Kṣattriya, its colour blood-red, its patron deity the Primal Tortoise (Kurmāvatāra of Vishnu). Usage: scratching the head, theft, Narasiṃha, face of a deer, lion, monkey, tortoise, *karṇikara*, breast, fear, Kṣattṛiya caste, blood-red colour.

*Bāṇa* (arrow): the three fingers joined just touch the thumb, and the little finger is extended. Usage: the number six, Nāla-nṛtya.

*Ardha-sūcika* (half-needle): the forefinger of the Kapittha hand is raised. Usage: sprout, young bird, etc., large insect.

*Combined Hands* (samyutta hastāni):

Twenty-four combined Hands are exhibited as follows: Añjali, Kapota, Karkaṭa, Svastika, Ḍola, Puṣpapuṭa, Utsanga, Śiva-linga, Kaṭaka-vardhana, Kartarī-svastika, Śakaṭa, Śankha, Cakra, Sampuṭa, Pāśa, Kīlaka, Matsya, Kūrma, Varāha, Garuḍa, Nāga-bandha, Khaṭvā, Bheruṇḍa, Avahittha.

According to another book: when two Single Hands are combined, that is a Combined Hand. Even though the origin and meaning remain the same, the patron deity always differs.

*Añjali* (salutation): two Patāka hands are joined palm to palm. Usage: saluting Deities, Elders (*guru*) or Brāhmaṇas — the hands being held on the head for Deities, before the face for Elders, and on the chest for Brāhmaṇas.

According to another text: same definition. The patron deity is Kṣetrapāla. Usage: bowing, obedience, clapping time, indicating the form of Śiva, saying " What am I to do ? ", meditation. (Plate VIII.)

*Kapota* (dove): the hands are joined at the side, base and top. Usage: taking oath, conversation with elders etc., humble acquiescence.

According to another book: the Añjali hands are separated. The patron deity is Citrasena. Usage: acquiescence, trees such as the coconut, areca-nut, etc., plantain flower, cold, nectar, receiving things, casket, citron.

*Karkaṭa* (crab): the fingers of the hands are interlocked, and the hands turned inwards or outwards.[1] Usage: group, stoutness, blowing the conch, stretching the limbs, bending the bough of a tree.

According to another book: in the Urṇa-nābha hand, the fingers of one hand are introduced into the interspaces of those of the other hand. Its patron deity is Vishnu. Usage: lamentation, yawning, breathing hard, crab, blowing the conch, cracking the fingers by women. (Plates IV A, extreme left, and XII E.)

[1] i. e. ' clasped hands '; but the hands may also be flattened by extending the elbows, the fingers remaining interlocked, and this is used in stretching the arms over the head, a sign of amorous feeling frequently mentioned in literature and depicted in painting and sculpture (Plate IV A, extreme left).

*Svastika* (crossed): two Patāka hands held together at the wrists. Usage: crocodile, timid speech, ḍispute, praising.

*Ḍola* (swing)[1]: two Patāka hands placed on the thighs. Usage: beginning a Nāṭya.

According to another book: Patāka hands at the sides. The patron deity is Bharatī. Usage: infatuation, fainting, drunken indolence, welcoming the beloved (*vilāsa*), etc.

*Puṣpapuṭa* (flower-casket): Sarpa-śīrṣa hands are pressed together. Usage: offering lights (*ārati*), twilight water-offering (*sandhya argha dāna*), flower-spells (*mantra-puṣpa*), children receiving fruits, etc.

According to another book: one Sarpa-śīrṣa hand by the side of the other. The patron deity is Kinnareśvara. Usage: offering and receiving flowers, corn, fruits, or water.

*Utsanga* (embrace): Mṛga-śīrṣa hands held upon opposite armpits. Usage: embrace, modesty, armlet, education of children.

According to another book: Arāla hands held crosswise on the shoulders. The patron deity is Gautama. Usage: modesty, embrace, assent, cold, saying " Sādhu ", hiding the breasts, etc.

*Śiva-linga* (do.): Ardha-candra with the left hand, Śikhara with the right. Usage: Śiva-linga.

*Kaṭaka-vardhana* (link of increase): Kaṭaka-mukha hands with crossed wrists. Usage: coronation, ritual (*pūja*), marriage blessing.

According to another book: Kaṭaka hands are crossed. The patron deity is Yakṣa-rāja. Usage: ḍeliberation (*vicāra*), the erotic flavour (*śṛngara rasa*), pacification, (the dances known as) Jakkiṇī naṭana and Daṇḍa lāsya, certainty.

*Kartarī-svastika* (crossed arrow-shafts): Kartarī-mukha hands are crossed. Usage: trees, the boughs of trees, the summit of a hill.

*Śakaṭa* (car): Bhramara hands with the thumb and middle finger extended. Usage: the gestures of Rākṣasas.

[1] Apparently identical with the *Kaṭyavalambita* hand of T. A. Gopinatha Rao, " Hindu Iconography," Vol. I, pt. i, p. 16, and ibid., Pl. V, fig. 11.

*Śankha* (conch): the thumbs of Śikhara hands are joined, and the forefinger extended. Usage: conch.

*Cakra* (discus): Ardha-candra hands askew, the palms in contact. Usage: discus.

*Sampuṭa* (casket): the fingers of the Cakra hand are bent. Usage: concealing things, casket.

*Pāśa* (noose): the forefingers of the Sūci hand are bent and interlocked. Usage: enmity, noose, manacles. (Plate XII F.)

*Kīlaka* (bond): the little fingers of the Mṛga-śīrṣa hand are interlocked. Usage: affection, the conversation of lovers.

*Matsya* (fish): Patāka hands face downwards, the thumbs and little fingers extended.[1] Usage: fish. (Plate XIV C.)

*Kūrma* (tortoise): the ends of the fingers of the Cakra hand are bent, except the thumbs and little fingers. Usage: tortoise. (Plate XIV D.)

*Varāha* (boar): Mṛga-śīrṣa hands one upon the other (back to back), the thumbs and little fingers linked. Usage: boar.

*Garuḍa:* Ardha-candra hands are held with palms askew, and the thumbs interlocked. Usage: Garuḍa. (Plate XIV E.)

*Nāga-bandha* (serpent-tie): Sarpa-śīrṣa hands are crossed. Usage: *nāga-bandha,* pairs of snakes, bower, Atharva Veda spells.

*Khaṭvā* (bed): the thumbs and forefingers of two Catura hands are left free. Usage: bed, etc. (Cf. Plate XIV B).

*Bheruṇḍa:* the wrists of Kapittha hands are joined. Usage: pair of Bheruṇḍas.

*Avahittha* (dissimulation): two Alapadma hands are held on the chest. Usage: erotic dances (*sṛngāra naṭana*), holding a play-ball, the breasts (Plates XI E, XIII D).

Such are the twenty-four Combined Hands in order.

According to another book the combined hands are as follows:

*Avahittha:* Śukatuṇḍa hands held against the heart. The patron deity is Mārkaṇḍeya. Usage: debility, wasting of the body, eager interest, thinness.

[1] The palm of one hand on the back of the other, the fingers along the fingers, and the two little fingers and thumbs moved to and fro.

*Gajadanta* (elephant's tusk):[1] Sarpa-śīrṣa hands, the middles of the arms boldly crossed. Patron deity Paramātmā. Usage: grasping a pillar, pulling up a stone, lifting anything heavy.

*Caturaśra* (square): Kaṭaka-mukha hands are held before the chest. Patron deity Varāhi. Usage: churning, Jakkiṇī naṭana, holding, milking, covering with cloths, wearing pearls, dragging ropes, tying the girdle, tying the bodice, holding flowers, etc., plying the fly-whisk.

*Tala-mukha* (palms facing): two hands raised face to face before the chest, (not touching). Patron deity Vijñarāja. Usage: embrace, stout things, a thick pillar, a sweet-sounding drum.

*Svastika* (crossed): Tripatāka hands crossed on the left side. Patron deity Guha. Usage: Wishing-tree, mountains.

*Āviddha-vakra* (swinging curve): *vyāvṛtta* Patāka hands are shown with grace and with (movement of) the elbows. Patron deity Tumburu. Usage: tying the girdle, difference, slenderness of waist, folk dances (*deṣya naṭana*).

*Recita:* Haṃsa-pakṣa hands face upwards, held apart. Patron deity Yakṣarāja. Usage: holding children, showing a painted panel (*citra-phalaka*).

*Nitamba* (buttock): Patāka hands face upwards, turned over, (extended from) the shoulder to the buttocks. Patron deity Agastya. Usage: weariness, descent or entry (*avataraṇa*), astonishment, ecstasy, etc.

*Latā* (creeper): Patāka hands held like a swing. Patron deity Śakti. Usage: being heavy with drink, beginning (the dance called) *svabhāva naṭana*, lines, state of union (*yoga*-condition), etc.

*Pakṣa-vañcita* (bent wing): Tripatāka hands are placed upon the hips. Patron deity Arjuna. Usage: movement of the thighs, difference.

*Pakṣa-pradyota* (shining wing): Pakṣa-vañcita hands face upwards. Patron deity Siddha. Usage: despondence, loss of wits, strangeness, magic boar, pot gesture (*kumbhābhinaya*).

[1] Quite distinct from the *Gaja* or *Daṇḍa* hand of T. A. Gopinatha Rao, "Hindu Iconography", Vol. I, pt. i, p. 16, and ibid., Pl. V, fig. 12, illustrated here on Plates I and III.

*Garuḍa-pakṣa* (Garuḍa wing): Ardha-candra hands held at the sides of the hips, extended upwards. Patron deity Sanandana. Usage: waist string, superiority.

*Niṣedha* (defence): the Mukula hand enclosed by the Kapittha hand. Patron deity Tumburu. Usage: establishing the conclusion of an argument, truth, saying "Verily", holding the nipples, *anga-pūja*.

*Makara:* Ardha-candra hands, one enclosing the other, palms downwards, the thumbs moving. Patron deity Mahendra. Usage: the sea, overflowing of a river, deer-face, prosperity, solidity, platform, crocodile.

*Vardhamāna* (increase): Haṃsa-pakṣa hands palms down, turned together face upwards. Patron deity Vāsuki. Usage: Narasiṃha, his glory, tearing the rākṣasa's chest.

*Udvṛtta* (asunder): one Haṃsa-pakṣa hand held face downwards and one face upwards. Patron deity Vāsiṣṭha. Usage: modesty, simile, torment, thorns etc., difference, consideration.

*Viprakīrna* (loosed): Svastika hands quickly separated. Patron deity Dakṣina-mūrti. Usage: drawing away the end of the robe (*celāñcala*), releasing.

*Arāla-kaṭaka-mukha:* Arāla and Kaṭaka-mukha hands held crossed. Patron deity Vāmana. Usage: giving pieces of betel leaf, anxiety, dismay.

*Sūcyāsya* (needle-face): Sūci hands are moved aside from the front simultaneously. Patron deity Nārada. Usage: saying "What am I to do?", yearning for the beloved, saying "Everything", or "Look here."

*Ardha-recita:* of two Recita hands one is held palm downwards. Patron deity Nandikeśvara. Usage: invitation, giving presents, concealing actions.

*Keśa-bandha* (tying the hair): Patāka hands binding the hair. Patron deity Durgā. Usage: gem-pillar, binding the hair, cheek, etc.

*Muṣṭi-svastika* (crossed fists): Muṣṭi hands are crossed on the stomach. Patron deity Kiṃpuruṣa. Usage: playing ball, boxing, great bashfulness, tying the girdle.

*Nalinī-padmakośa:* Padmakośa hands are outward-turned and crossed. Patron deity Śeṣa. Usage: *nāga-bandha*, buds, making equal distribution, cluster of flowers, the number ten, Gaṇḍa-bheruṇḍa. (Identical with Nalina-padmakośa; Introduction, pp. 4, 5.)

*Udveṣṭitālapadma:* Alapadma hands are held on the chest and twisted upwards. Patron deity Śakti. Usage: husband, humble words, the breasts, full-blown lotus, saying "I am beloved", conversation, indicating desires. (Plates XI E, XIII D.)

*Ulbaṇa* (abundance): the same hands held close to the eyes. Patron deity Vijñeśa. Usage: large clusters of flowers, eyes.

*Lālita:* the same hands crossed near the head. Patron deity Vaiṣṇavī. Usage: *sāl*-tree, mountain.

According to a different book the Combined Hands are as follows:

Twenty-seven hands are described as follows: Viprakīrṇa, Tala-mukha, Gajadanta, Sūci-viddha, Pallava, Nitamba, Keśa-bandha, Latā, Dvirada, Uddhṛta, Samyama, Mudrā, Aja-mukha, Ardha-mukula, Recita, Kuśala, Pakṣa-vañcita, Tilaka, Utthāna-vañcita, Vardhamāna, Jñāna, Rekhā, Vaiṣṇava, Brahmokta-śukatuṇḍa, Khaṇḍa-catura, Ardha-catura, Līna-mudrā. [The descriptions in many cases correspond with what has already been given.]

*Eleven Hands denoting Relationships:*

*Dampati* (husband and wife): left hand Śikhara, right hand Mṛga-śīrsa, indicating female and male.

*Mātṛ* (mother): left hand Ardha-candra, right hand Saṃdaṃsa, the left hand then placed on the stomach, showing the Strī hand[1]; indicating mother or daughter.

*Pitṛ* (father): following the last hand, the right hand is held as Śikhara; indicating father or son-in-law.

*Śvaśṛ* (mother-in-law): the right hand is held as Haṃsāsya and Saṃdaṃsa at the throat, the left hand then placed on the stomach showing the Strī hand.

[1] The Strī (woman) hand is not separately described, but it will be seen that it consists in placing either hand on the stomach, indicating the womb.

*Śvaśura* (father-in-law): following the last hand, the right hand is shown as Śikhara.

*Bhartr-bhrātṛ* (brother-in-law): the left hand Śikhara, the right hand Kartarī-mukha at the side.

*Nananda* (sister-in-law): following the Bhartṛ-bhrātṛ hand the Strī hand is shown with the left.

*Jyeṣṭa kaniṣṭha bhrātṛ* (elder or younger brother): the Mayura hand shown forwards and backwards.

*Snuṣa* (daughter-in-law): following the last, the Strī hand is shown with the right.

*Bhartṛ* (husband): Haṃsāsya and Śikhara hands are held at the throat.

*Sapatni* (co-wife): the Pāśa hand is shown first, and then Strī with both hands.

Thus are described in order the eleven hands denoting relationships. Those not mentioned are to be inferred according to circumstances.

*Hands that indicate the forms which accord with the character and actions of Brahmā and other Devas:* [1]

*Brahmā:* l. h. Catura, r. h. Haṃsāsya.
*Śambhu:* l. h. Mṛga-śīrṣa, r. h. Tripatāka.
*Vishnu:* Tripatāka with both hands.
*Sarasvatī:* l. h. Ardha-candra, r. h. Sūci.
*Pārvatī:* Ardha-candra with both hands, the left upward, the right downward, making Abhaya and Varada (Fear not, and Charity).
*Lakṣmī:* two Kapittha hands held at the shoulders.[2]
*Vijñeśvara:* two Kapittha hands held forward.
*Śanmukha:* l. h. Triśūla, r. h. Śikhara, held upwards.
*Manmatha:* l. h. Śikhara, r. h. Kaṭaka.
*Indra:* Tripatāka hands crossed.
*Yama:* l. h. Pāśa, r. h. Sūci.
*Nairṛti:* Khaṭvā and Śakaṭa hands.

[1] Showing Deva hands is referred to in a subsequent section as '*deva-vibhāvana*.'

[2] 'Held at the shoulders' is to be understood in the case of all the Deva hands unless otherwise indicated.

*Varuṇa:* l. h. Śikhara, r. h. Patāka.
*Vayu:* l. h. Ardha-patāka, r. h. Arāla.
*Kuvera:* l. h. Padma, r. h. Gada.

*Hands that indicate the Nine Planets* (nava graha).

*Sūrya:* Solapadma and Kapittha hands held on the shoulders.
*Candra:* l. h. Solapadma, r. h. Patāka.
*Angārakha:* l. h. Sūci, r. h. Muṣṭi.
*Budha:* l. h. Muṣṭi askew, r. h. Patāka.
*Bṛhaspati:* Śikhara with both hands, as if holding the sacred thread.
*Śukra:* Muṣṭi with both hands, the left raised, the right downwards.
*Śanaiscara:* l. h. Sarpa-śīrṣa, r. h. Triśūla.
*Rahu:* l. h. Sarpa-śīrṣa, r. h. Sūci.
*Ketu:* l. h. Sūci, r. h. Ardha-patāka.

*Hands of the Ten Avatārs of Vishnu.*

*Matsya:* the Matsya hand is shown, then both hands Tripatāka level at the shoulders.
*Kūrma:* the Kūrma hand is shown, then both hands Tripatāka level at the shoulders.
*Narasiṃha:* l. h. Siṃha-mukha, r. h. Tripatāka.
*Vāmana:* Muṣṭi with both hands, one upwards and the other downwards, and towards the right side.
*Paraśurāma:* the left hand on the hip and Ardha-patāka with the right.
*Raghurāma:* r. h. Kapittha, l. h. Śikhara, held respectively near and far.
*Balarāma:* l. h. Muṣṭi, r. h. Patāka.
*Krishna:* Mṛga-śīrṣa hands facing one another on the shoulders.
*Kalki:* l. h. Tripatāka, r. h. Patāka.

(Buddha is omitted.)
The Rākṣasa Hand: Both hands Śakaṭa, held on the face.

*Hands denoting the Four Castes:*

*Brāhmaṇa:* Śikhara with both hands, as if holding the sacred thread, the right hand moved to and fro.

*Kṣattriya:* Śikhara with the left hand moved to and fro, Patāka with the right.
*Vaiṣya:* l. h. Haṃsāsya, r. h. Kaṭaka.
*Śūdra:* l. h. Śikhara, r. h. Sūci.

The Hands of the Eighteen other Castes are shown according to their work. In the same way the hands are to be inferred which indicate the people of different countries.

There are as many hands as meanings. Their usage is to be regulated by their literal meaning, category, gender, and suitability. So much is told in an abridged form, following careful research; those who are acquainted with the moods of the heart should use the hands with due care after consulting the texts, as may be required.

The following are mentioned in another book:

*Hands of Famous Emperors.* — *Hariscandra*, Śukaṭuṇḍa. *Nala*, Mayura. *Purukutsa*, Alapadma. *Purūravas*, Muṣṭi. *Sagara*, Alapadma on the head. *Dilīpa*, Patāka. *Ambariṣa*, Kartarī. *Śibi*, Kapittha hand waved forwards. *Kārttivīrya*, two Patāka hands at the shoulders in *deva-vibhāvana*. *Rāvaṇa*, the same hands with widely separated fingers, feathered. *Dharmarāja*, hands waved near the arms. *Arjuna*, Tripatāka moved forward again and again. *Bhīma*, Muṣṭi hand moved forward. *Śaibya*, Sūci hand with the finger twisted upward. *Nakula*, Kaṭaka. *Sahadeva*, Śikhara. *Nahusa*, the hand moving. *Yayāti*, Tāmracūda. *Bhagīratha*, Ardha-candra hand made like Tripatāka, and this is also used for an eclipse of the moon (lit. seizing by Rahu).

For the Lords of the Earth *Mandhātā* and *Marutvān*, Mukula, Sūci and Muṣṭi hands and the Ardha-patāka twisted upwards touching the body, these four hands are used in order. For the great Kings *Raghu* and *Aja*, Ardha-patāka hands as aforesaid are used respectively right and left. *Daśaratha*, Ardha-patāka hands crossed. For *Rāma* the Śikhara hand, and also for other kings who bear the bow. For *Bharata*, Śikhara hand held on the right shoulder. For *Lakṣmaṇa*, the same on the left shoulder. For *Satrughna*, the same on the face. If these are done with the left hand on the left shoulder, it indicates those of the Lunar race.

*Hands of the Seven Oceans:*

*Lavaṇa:* Mukula hands moved upwards and downwards (*vyāvṛttacāpaveṣṭitau*).[1]

*Ikṣu:* Alapadma hands in the same way.

*Sūra:* Sankīrṇa and Patāka hands in the same manner.

*Sarpi:* Catura (hands in the same manner).

*Dadhi:* Tripatāka hands in the same manner.

*Kṣīra:* Sarpa-śīrṣa hands in the same manner.

*Suddhodaka* (Jala): Patāka hands held just as before.

*Hands of the Famous Rivers.*—Moving upwards and downwards (*vyāvṛttacāpaveṣṭitau*) indicates a river, etc.: for any river, the Patāka hand is used. I shall expound the right fashion of those hands that indicate Gangā, etc., in accordance with their special virtues.

For *Gangā*, etc., Tāmracūḍa; for *Yamunā*, Rekhā; for *Kṛṣṇāverī*, Siṃha-mukha; *Kaverī*, Catura; *Sarasvatī*, Patāka and Catura; *Narmadā*, Ardha-patāka; *Tungabhadra*, Haṃsāsya; *Śarasvatī*, Bāṇa; *Vetrāvatī*, Sūci; *Candra-bhāga* (Chenab) the hand moving; *Śarayu*, Padma; *Bhīmarathi*, Arāla; *Suvarṇamukhī*, Ardha-catura; *Pāpanāsinī*, Śukatuṇḍa. So it is said by those who know *bhāva*; and for rivers not mentioned here the Patāka hand is applicable.

*The Upper Worlds.*—For the Seven Upper Worlds, *Bhu, Bhuvar, Svarga, Jana, Tapa, Satya, Mahar,* the Patāka hand twisted upwards is applicable.

*The Lower Worlds.*—For the Seven Lower Worlds, *Atala, Vitala, Sutala, Talātala, Mahātala, Rasātala,* and *Pātāla,* the Patāka hand twisted downwards is applicable.

*Hands indicating Trees.*—*Aśvattha* (pipal), Alapadma hands, waving the fingers; *Kadalī*, Mukula hands interlocked, extended, and the fingers waved; *Nārangi* (orange), Padmakośa; *Lakuca*, Bhramara; *Panasa* (bread-fruit), Catura; *Vilva* (wood-apple), the same; *Punnāga*, Patāka and Catura; *Mandāra*, Khaṇḍa-catura; *Vakula*, Saṃdaṃsa; *Vata* (banyan), Patāka; *Arjuna*, Siṃha-mukha; *Pāṭalī*, Śukatuṇḍa; *Hintāla*, Kartarī-mukha;

[1] Representing the up and down motion of waves.

*Pūga* (areca-nut), Padmakośa hands crossed; *Campaka*, Lāngula hand downwards; *Khadira*, Tāmracūḍa quite face downwards; *Śamī*, Kartarī hands interlocked; *Aśoka*, Patāka hands crossed, i. e. touching at the wrists and freely moving to and fro; *Sindhuvāra*, Mayura hands interlocked; *Āmalaka*, the Samyama Nāyaka hand, i. e. the forefinger and second finger together in the middle of the palm, the rest extended; *Kuruvaka*, Kartarī and Tripatāka hands; *Kapittha* (elephant-apple), Alapadma hands are crossed; *Ketakī* (screw-pine), Patāka and Catura hands crossed at the wrists; *Śimśapa*, Ardha-candra hands crossed; *Nimbasala*, Śukatuṇḍa hands crossed; *Pārijāta*, the Trijñāna hand, i. e. Patāka with both hands twisted upwards; *Tintrini*, Lāngula hand; *Jambu*, the Ardha-patāka hand; *Pālāsa*, the Ardha-candra hand; *Rasāla* (mango), the Tripatāka hand.

*Hands that indicate the Lion and other Animals.*—Lion, the Siṃha-mukha hand, i. e., r. h. Siṃha-mukha, and l. h. Patāka applied to the back of the right, the fingers being freely moved; Tiger, the Ardha-candra hand held face downwards; Boar, the Sankīrṇa-makara hand, i. e. in the aforesaid Matsya hand, the r. h. is held downwards and shaken, the five fingers being severally held apart, indicating bristles; Monkey, the Adho-muṣṭi-mukula hand is used, i. e. the thumb and second finger of the Muṣṭi hand are joined; Bear, l. h. Padmakośa face downwards, r. h. Patāka placed on the back of the left; Cat, the Ardha-mukula hand, i. e. the thumb and third finger of the Muṣṭi hand are joined; Yak, the hands touching at the wrists, l. h. Muṣṭi, r. h. Mudrikā, making the Muṣṭi-mudrā hand; Iguana, Tala-patāka hand, i. e. the thumb and little finger of the Patāka hand are slightly raised; Porcupine Deer, the Candra-mṛga hand, i. e. the forefinger of the Mṛga hand is raised; Antelope, the Mṛga-śīrṣa hand; Black Antelope, the Muṣṭi-mrga hand, i. e. the thumb and little finger of the Muṣṭi hand are extended; Mule, Nāga-bandha hands directed upwards, indicating 'Cow-ear'; Mouse, the Khaṇḍa-mukula hand, i. e. the forefinger of the Mukula hand is fully extended; Mole (?) (girikā), the Khaḍga-mukula hand, i. e. the forefinger of the Mukula hand is bent and moved to and fro (*tiryak prasārita*); Hare, the Tala-patāka hand is moved horizontally (*tiryak*); Scorpion, the Karkaṭa hand is directed downwards; Dog, the Madhya-patāka hand, i. e. the little finger of the Patāka hand is bent; Camel, the Kaṇḍāñjali hand, i. e. the thumbs of the Añjali hand are bent and moved up and down; Goat, Śikhara hands in contact face to face; Ass, the Bhinnāñjali hand, i. e. the forefingers of the Khaṇḍāñjali hand are bent in contact; Bull, the Tala-siṃha[1] hand, i. e. the second and third fingers are bent to touch the palm, and the thumb placed over them, and the two other fingers extended; Cow, the Sankīrṇa-mudrā hand, i. e. the middle finger is bent, and all the others extended, also indicating *Yantra-bheda*.

*Hands that indicate Flying Creatures.* — Dove, the Kapota hand fluttered (*punkhita*); Pigeon, the same hand moved horizontally (*tiryak*); Hawk, Śukatuṇḍa hand; Owl, Gaja-danta hands face to face in contact; *Gaṇḍa-bheruṇḍa*, Ardha-candra hands face downwards, touching at the wrists, and all the fingers separated; *Cātaka*, the Lāngula hand fluttered; Cock, the Bhramara hand; *Kokila*, the Arāla hand fluttered; Crow, the Saṃdaṃsa-mukula hand, i. e. the forefinger of the Bhramara hand is placed on the thumb, and the hand fluttered; Osprey, the Sūci hand relaxed (*apaviddha*); Parrot, the Śukatuṇḍa hand fluttered; Crane (*sārasa*), the Pradiṣa-mukula hand, i. e. the Mukula hand with the little finger slightly bent; Crane (*baka*), the mingled-Haṃsa hand, i. e. the forefinger and thumb are joined, the second and third fingers extended, and the little finger made to touch the palm, this is also used in *Mantra-bheda*; Curlew, the Līnālapadma hand is used, i. e. the little finger of the Alapadma hand is bent to touch the palm; Firefly, the Haṃsa-mukha hand, i. e. the thumb is joined to the topmost joint of the middle finger, and the hand relaxed; Bee, the Bhramara hand fluttered; Swan (*haṃsa*), the Haṃsāsya hand; *Cakravāka*, Alapadma hands fluttered; Paddy-bird (*koyaṣṭika*), the Arāla-patāka hand, i. e. Arāla with the right hand, Patāka with the left, and the hands touching; *Vyāli*, the Vyāli hand,

[1] i. e. *Siṃha-mukha*, with the back of the hand in the horizontal plane. Plate XIII A.

i. e. the forefinger and middle finger bent like a bow, the third finger placed at the base of the thumb, the little finger bent.

*Hands that indicate Water-Animals.* — Frog, the double Cakra hand, i. e. the thumb and forefinger go in, the middle finger is bent, and the little finger extended; Crab, the Līna-karkaṭa hand, i. e., r. h. Karkaṭa direct upwards and placed on the l. h., the fingers being interlocked; Leech, Sūci hands moved along; Crocodile, Patāka hands crossed and held apart, also indicating a box; *Duṇḍupha*, the Kartarī-daṇḍa hand, i. e., r. h. Kartarī, face upwards, placed on the other fore-arm, and l. h. Kaṭaka-mukha.

This Mirror of Gesture has been edited by Tiruvenkaṭācāri of Niḍāmangalam, a very learned interpreter of Gesture and the like, according to the Bharata Śāstra, and into this work are likewise introduced many extracts from the Bharata Śāstra, for the pleasure of the cultivated public. Thus ends the Mirror of Gesture, with extracts from other books. *Śrī Sanātana-Rāma arpaṇam astu!*

## Works of Comparison and Reference

Coomaraswamy, Ananda, *Viśvakarmā*, London, 1915.

Coomaraswamy, Ananda, *The Arts and Crafts of India and Ceylon*, London, 1913.

Craig, Gordon, *The Art of the Theatre*, London, 2d ed. 1911.

Craig, Gordon, *The Mask*, 1900 ——

Foucher, *L'Iconographie Bouddhique*, Paris, 1910, 1911.

Fox-Strangways, A. H., *The Music of Hindustan*, Oxford, 1914.

Grosset, Joanny, *Bhāratīya-Nāṭya-Çāstram*, Tome I (all published), Paris, 1898.

Haas, O., *The Daśarūpa of Dhanaṃjaya*, New York, 1912.

Hincks, Marcelle A., *The Japanese Dance*, London, 1910.

India Society, *Ajanta Frescoes*, London, 1915.

Kakuzo, Okakura, *The Ideals of the East*, 2 ed., 1904. (Ashikaga Period.)

Knosp, Gaston, "Le Théâtre en Indo-Chine," *Anthropos*, 1908.

Leclère, Adhémard, "Le Théâtre Cambodgien," *Revue d'Ethnographie et de Sociologie*, 1911.

Lévi, Sylvain, *Le Théâtre Indien*, Paris, 1890.

Fenollosa, Ernest and Pound, Ezra, "*Noh*" *or Accomplishment*, London, 1917.

Pischel, R., *The Home of the Puppet-play* (translated by M. C. Tawney), London, 1912.

Rao, T. A. Gopinatha, *Hindu Iconography*, 1915.

Stopes, Marie C., *The Plays of Old Japan*, London, 1913.

Viśvanātha Kavirāja, *Sāhityadarpaṇa*, ed. with translation, Bibliotheca India, Calcutta, 1875.

# PLATES

THE COSMIC DANCE OF ŚIVA (NAṬARĀJA)

Copper figure in Madras Museum. The first right hand holding a drum, the second in *abhaya mudrā*, the first left hand (out of the picture, see Plate XI B) holding a flame, the forward left hand exhibiting the *gaja* or *daṇḍa* pose (cf. Plate III).

KURUKULLĀ

Nepalese copper figure, about sixteenth century, Calcutta Museum. Upper hands in position of shooting an arrow (Cf. Plate XV c).

DANSEUSE

Hands corresponding to the forward hands of Plate I. Buddhist frieze at Borobodur, Java, about ninth century, A.D.

A

B

C

CEILING SCULPTURE AT DILWARRA, MT. ĀBŪ

Dance with hand poses, and music.

DANSEUSES BEFORE A JAINA GODDESS
Ceiling sculpture at Dilwarra, Mt. Ābū.

APSARĀS DANCING
In the Vaikuṇṭha Sabhā of Vishnu: from an early Kāngrā painting in the collection of Mr. W. Rothenstein.

DANSEUSE

From an Ajaṇṭā fresco (sixth to seventh century A.D.): tracing by Samarendranath Gupta.

A. Buddha

Seated in *padmāsana*, the hands in *dharmacakra mudrā*.
Nepalese, eighth to ninth century.
(The r. h. alone is *haṃsāsya*.)
(Dr. Coomaraswamy's collection)

B. Bodhisattva

Seated in *lalitāsana*, the r. h. *tripatāka*, l. h. holding stalk of lotus.
(Javanese, ninth to eleventh century.)
(British Museum)

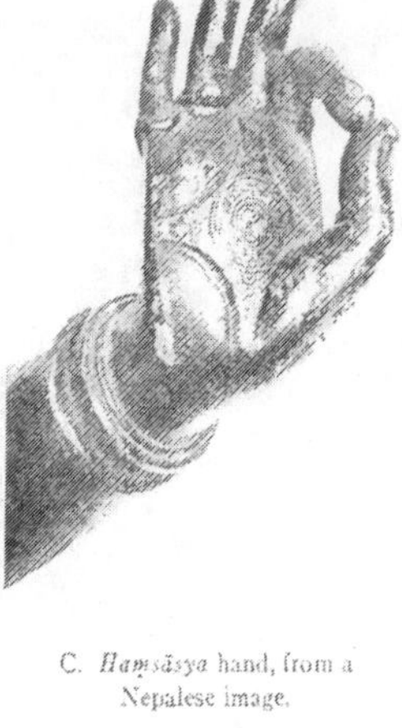

C. *Haṃsāsya* hand, from a Nepalese image.

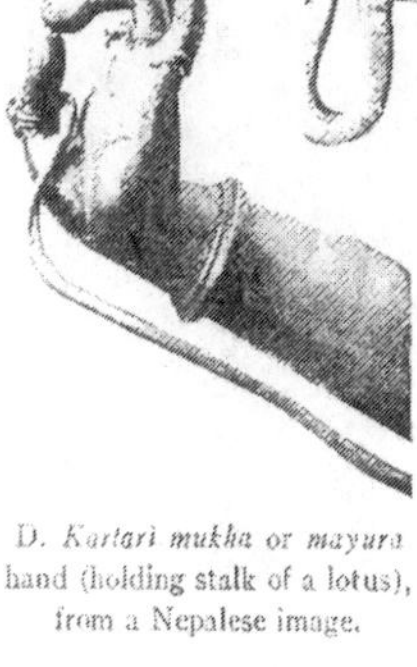

D. *Kartari mukha* or *mayura* hand (holding stalk of a lotus), from a Nepalese image.

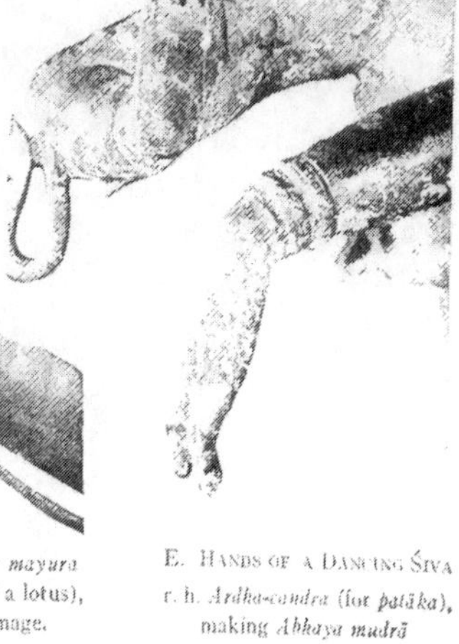

E. Hands of a Dancing Śiva
r. h. *Ardha-candra* (for *patāka*), making *Abhaya mudrā*

HANDS OF IMAGES

PLATE VIII

SEATED IMAGE WITH *AÑJALI* HANDS

COPPER GILT FIGURE OF A DONOR

Nepal, sixteenth to seventeenth century. Indian Museum, South Kensington, London.

NAUTCH DANCE BEFORE A ROYAL PATRON

From a sixteenth century Rājasthanī illustration of *Pañcama* (?) *rāgiṇi*, a musical mode, the dancer exhibiting *patāka* hands: chorus to left.

(Dr. Coomaraswamy's collection)

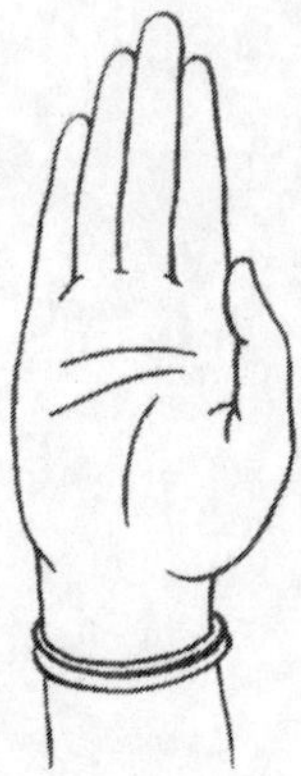

A. *Patāka* hand

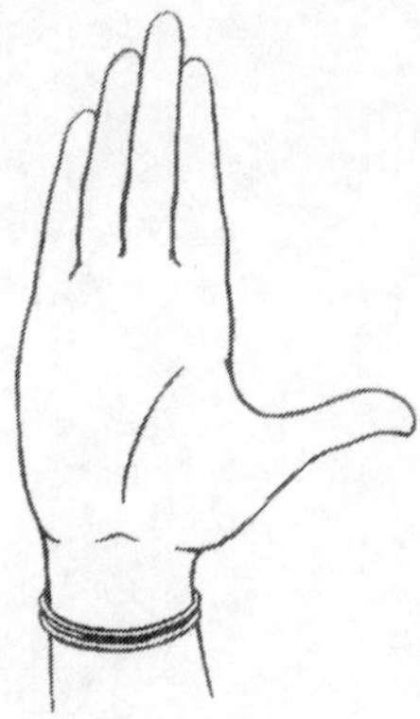

B. *Ardha-candra* hand

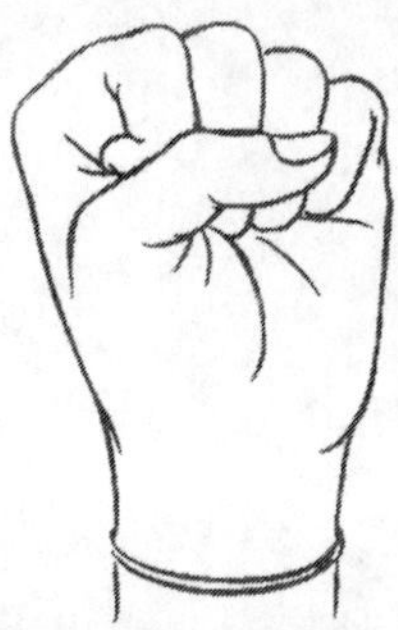

C. *Muṣṭi* hand

D. *Śikhara* hand

E. *Bhramara* hand

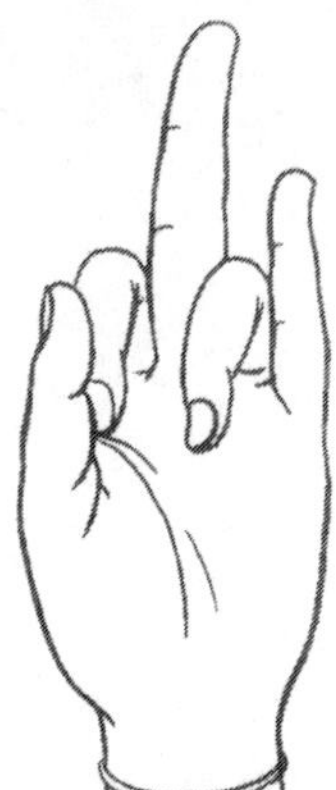

F. *Śukatuṇḍa* hand

SINGLE HANDS

(From drawings by Miss Dorothy M. Larcher.)

PLATE XI

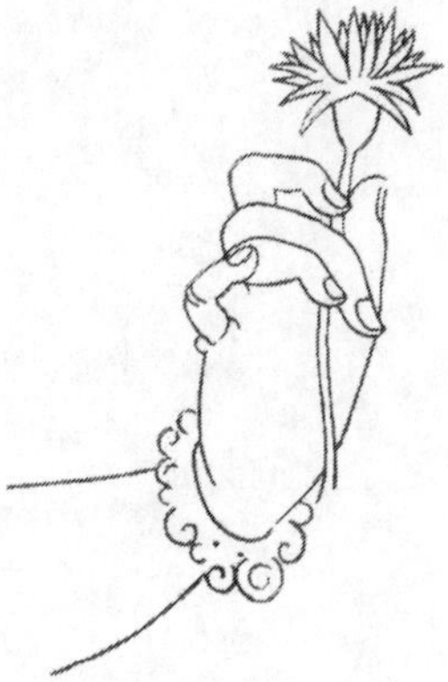

A. *Kaṭaka mukha* hand with blue lotus (hand of Bodhisattva, Ajaṇṭā).

B. *Ardha-candra* hand, with flame (upper left hand of figure represented on Pl. I).

C. *Kartar mukha* (hand of an image in Madras Museum).

D. *Padmakośa* hand.

E. *Udveṣṭitālapadma* hands.

SINGLE AND COMBINED HANDS

(D and E drawn by Miss Dorothy Larcher.)

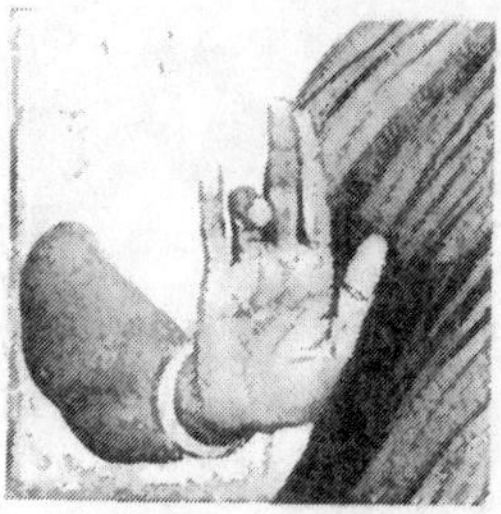

A. *Tripatāka* right hand

B. *Simha-mukha* left hand

C. *Alapadma* left hand

D. *Sikhara* left hand

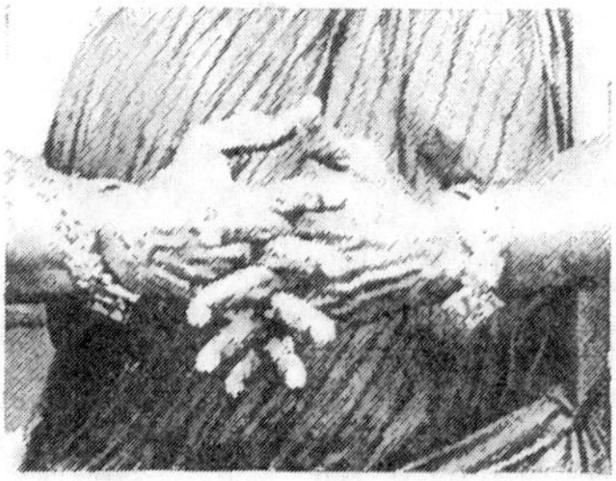

E. *Karkaṭa* combined hands (a grove of trees)

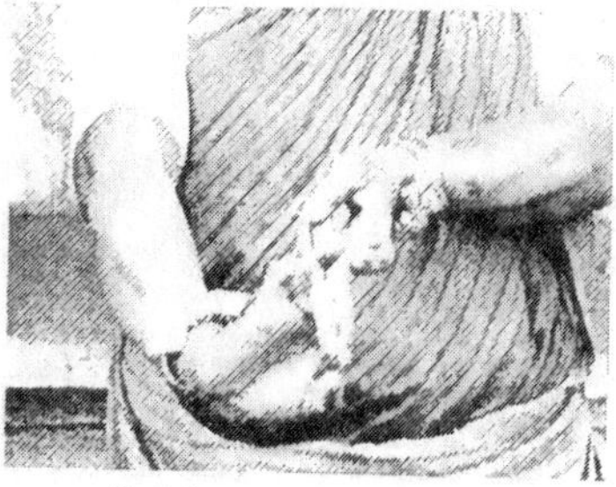

F. *Pāśa* combined hands (enmity)

SINGLE AND COMBINED HANDS

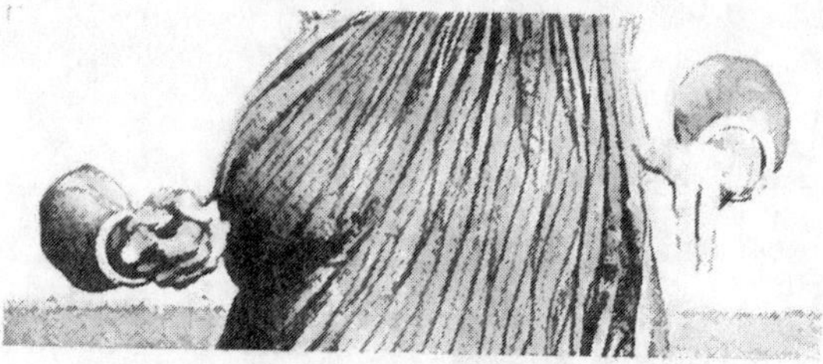

A. r. h. *Sūcī*, l. h. *Siṃha mukha* representing Krishna driving cattle.

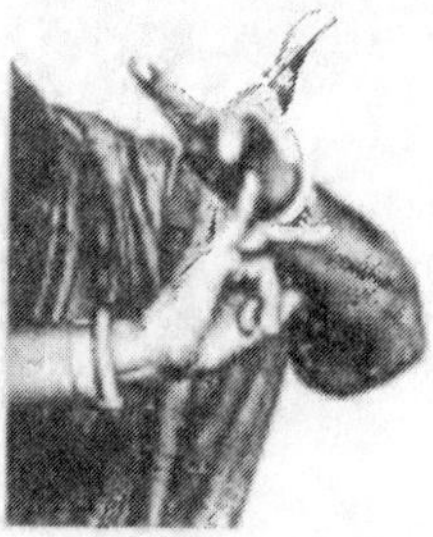

B. Raising Mt. Govardhan

C. The Rice-Mortar
(*Alapadma* hands)

D. Both Hands *udveṣṭitālapadma*

COMBINED HANDS

A. Eyebrows like the crescent moon (l. h. *candra-kalā*)

B. A Bed

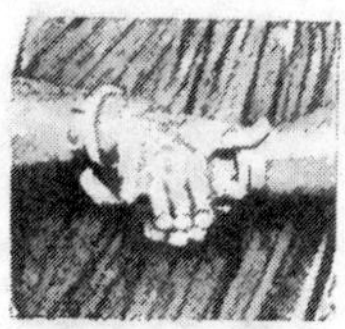

C. The Fish (Avatar of Vishnu)

The Tortoise (Avatar of Vishnu)

E. Garuḍa (Vehicle of Vishnu)

COMBINED HANDS